ARTIST TRANSCRIPTIONS® PIANO

HAMPTON HAWES Collection

ISBN 0-634-00003-9

HAL•LEONARD® CORPORATION

7777 W. BLUEMOUND RD. P.O. BOX 13819 MILWAUKEE, WI 53213

Visit Hal Leonard Online at
www.halleonard.com

Table of Contents

Biography/Discography

BIOGRAPHY

HAMPTON HAWES was born on November 13, 1928, the youngest of six children. His father was a minister and his mother played piano and organ for the church choir. When Hampton was very young, his mother would sit him on her lap with his hands on each of hers as she would practice. One day when she was talking on the phone to a friend, she was shocked when Hampton started playing the instrument on his own.

Hampton loved the music of the church, but he also loved jazz. Jazz was not acceptable to his father, and the boy was given clarinet lessons. These did not last long, and Hampton's father locked the piano to keep the boy from playing jazz. Hampton found the key and played the instrument when no one was home, re-locking it when he saw the family car pull into the driveway. At that time, he only played in the key of C.

He began playing professionally with Big Jay McNeely in 1944. He became part of the Central Avenue jazz scene in Los Angeles, playing with such legends as Red Norvo, Dexter Gordon, Teddy Edwards, Wardell Gray, and Johnny Otis. In 1947, he played with Charlie Parker's group for several months when Bird was living in California.

Hawes began leading his own groups after he served in the Army, recording a group of albums for the Contemporary label that remain some of the finest examples of piano jazz ever recorded. But in 1958, he was arrested on drug charges and spent four years in a government hospital.

After he was pardoned by President Kennedy, Hawes returned to leading a trio, but continued to experiment and stretch his musical language, often playing electric piano and synthesizer in later years. A career highlight was a world tour in 1967-8; Hawes recorded in Germany, France, Italy, Spain and Japan. He wrote an autobiography in 1974, *Raise Up Off Me*, and continued to develop and evolve as an artist until his death on May 22, 1977.

DISCOGRAPHY

All the Things You Are, Easy Living – LP: Contemporary C3505; CD: OJCCD-316

Autumn in New York, Stella by Starlight – LP: Contemporary C3515; CD: OJCCD-318

Body and Soul; I Remember You; Lover, Come Back to Me – LP: Contemporary C3523; CD: OJCCD-421

Fly Me to the Moon – LP: Moon 005 (+CD)

ALL THE THINGS YOU ARE

from VERY WARM FOR MAY

Lyrics by OSCAR HAMMERSTEIN II
Music by JEROME KERN

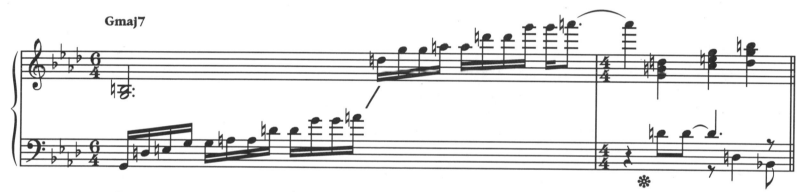

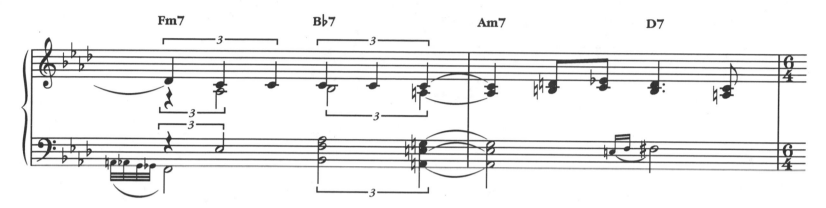

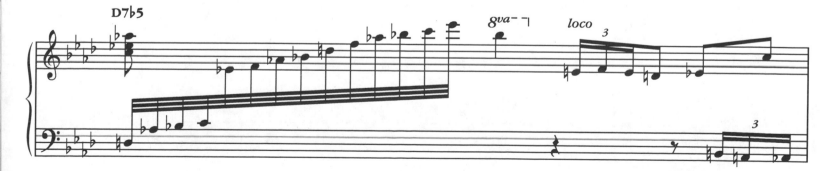

6

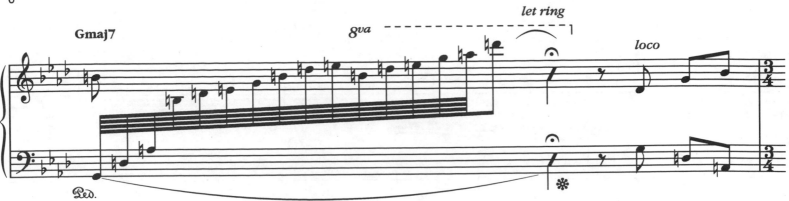

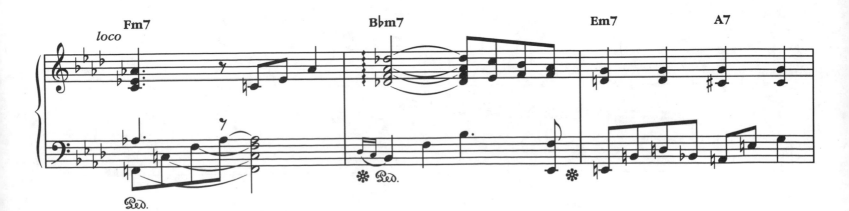

A♭maj7

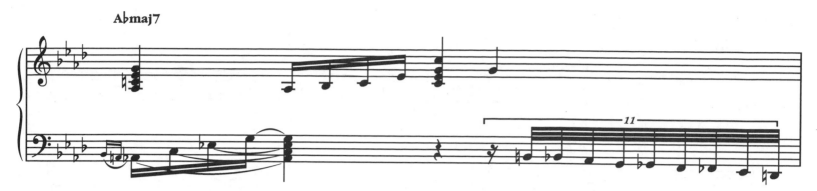

D♭maj7

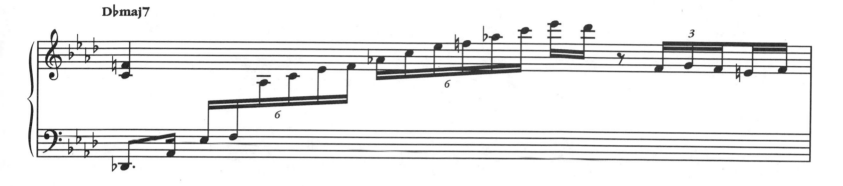

F♯13♯11

Cm7   **F7♯5(♯9)**   **B♭m7**

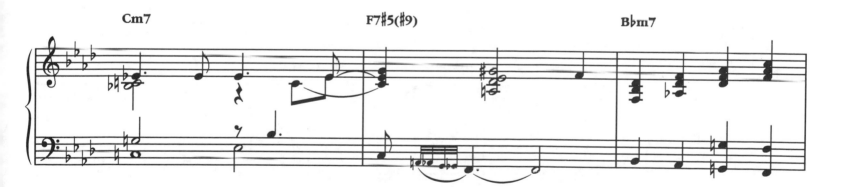

E♭7   **A♭/E♭**

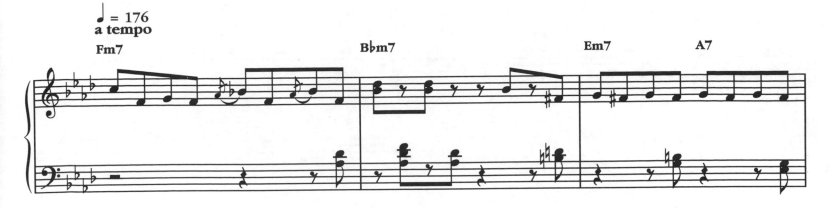

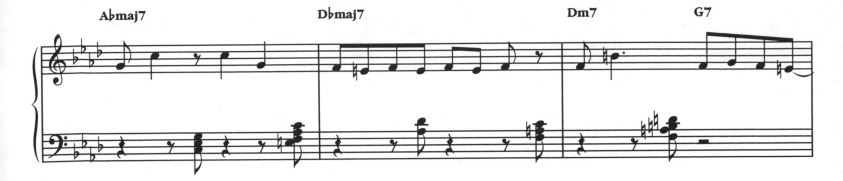

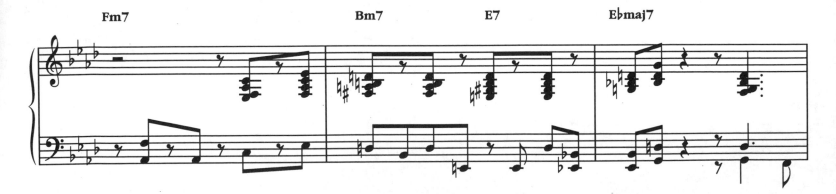

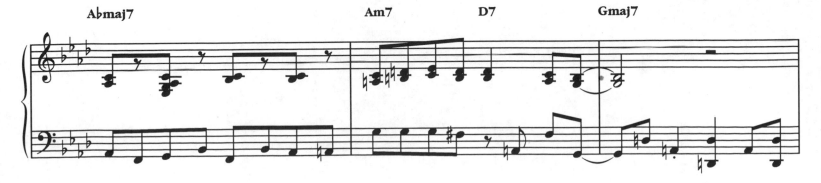

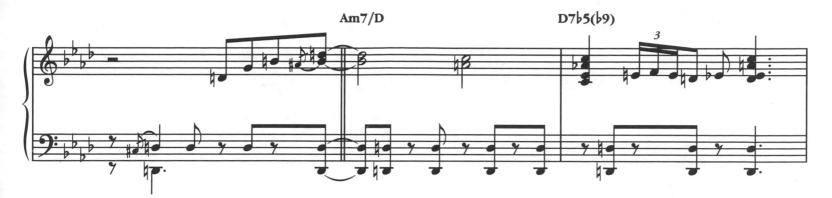

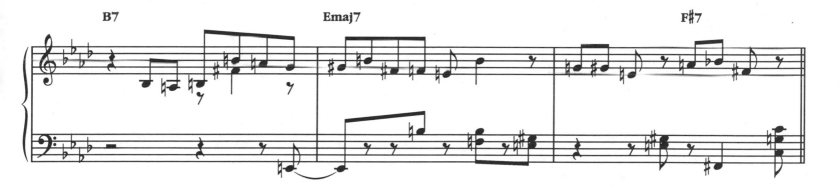

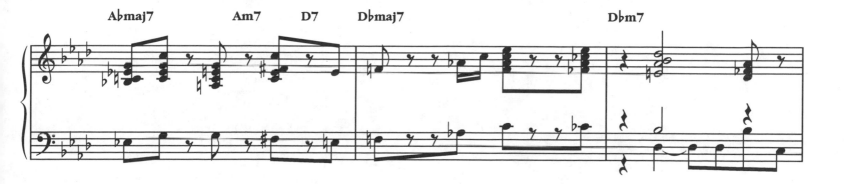

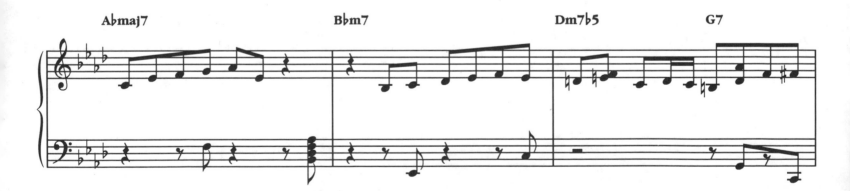

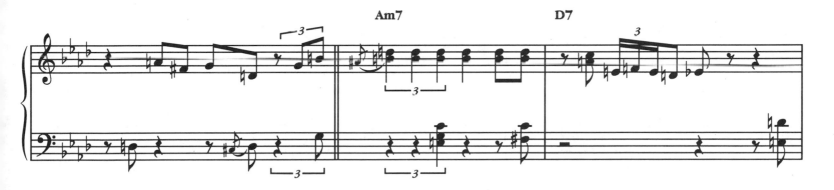

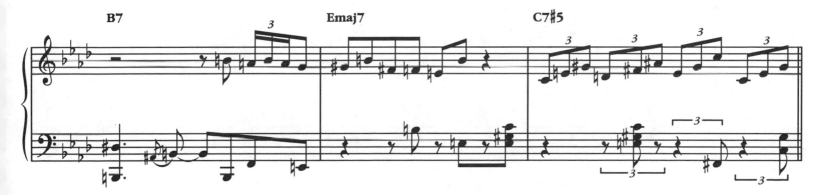

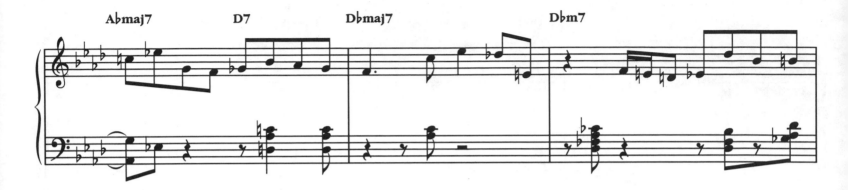

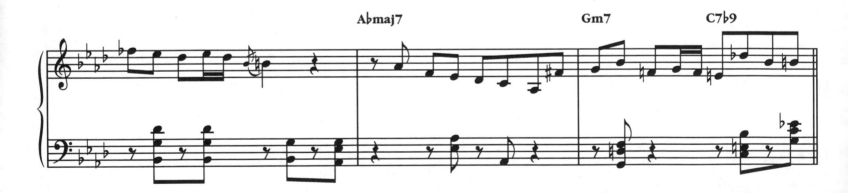

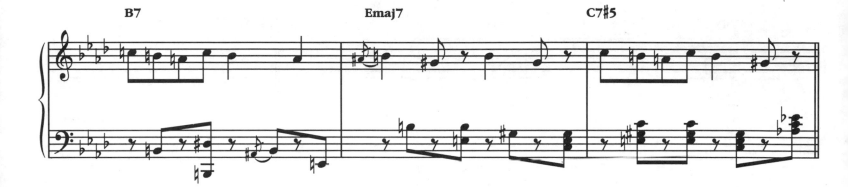

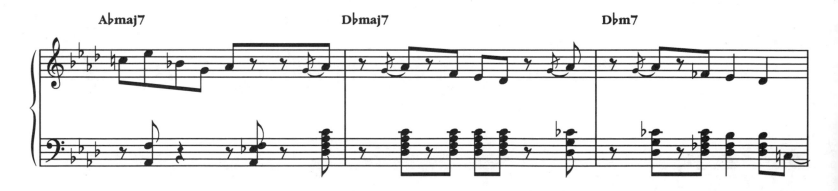

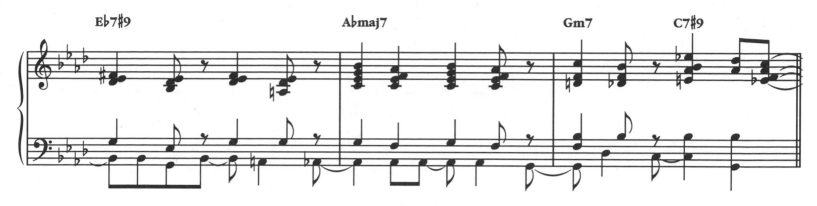

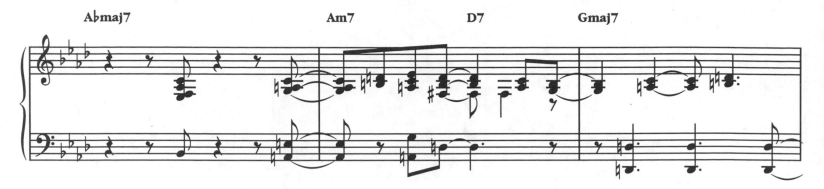

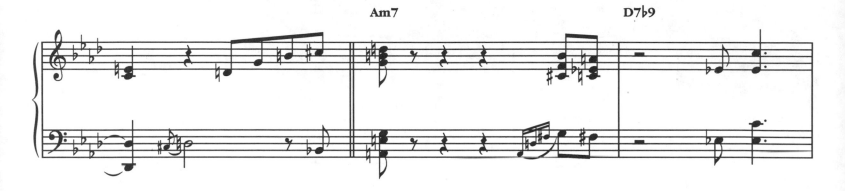

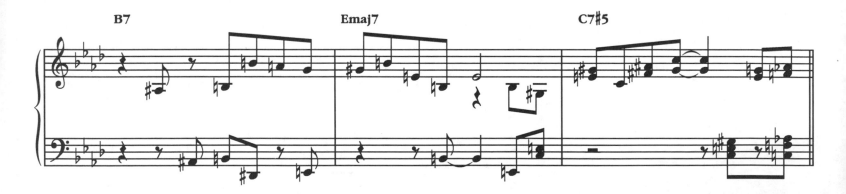

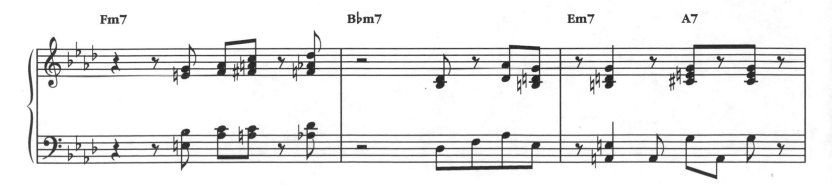

AUTUMN IN NEW YORK

Words and Music by
VERNON DUKE

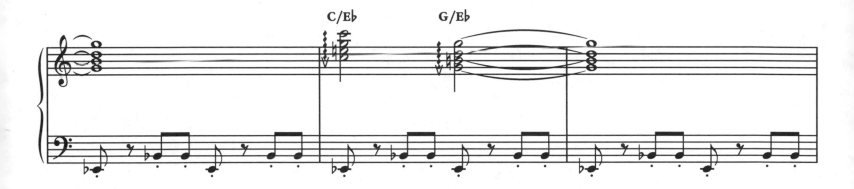

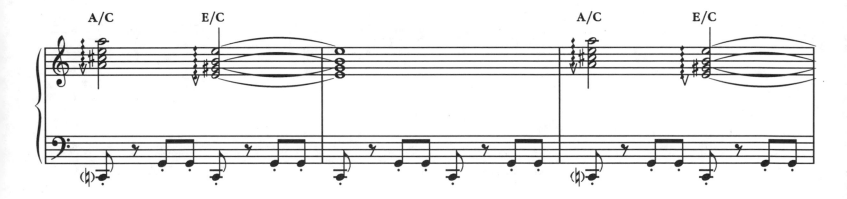

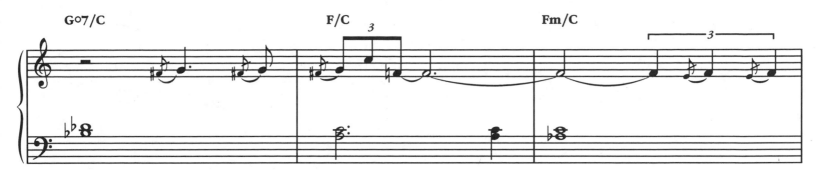

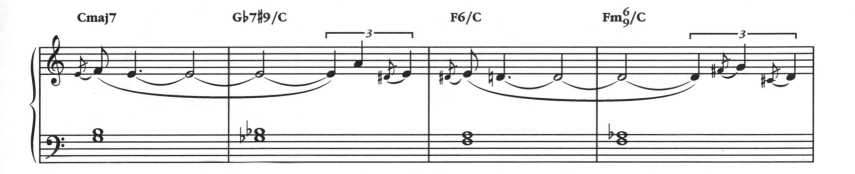

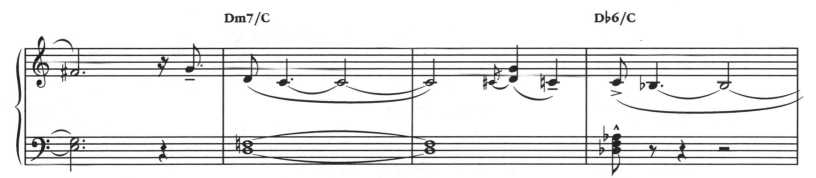

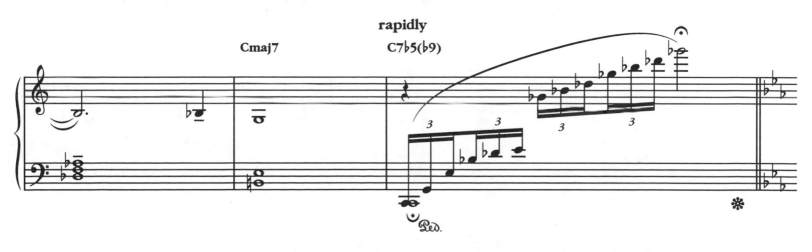

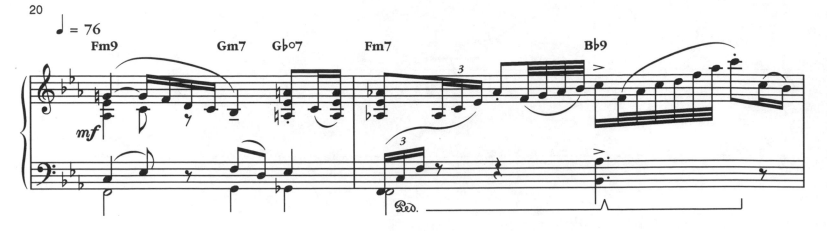

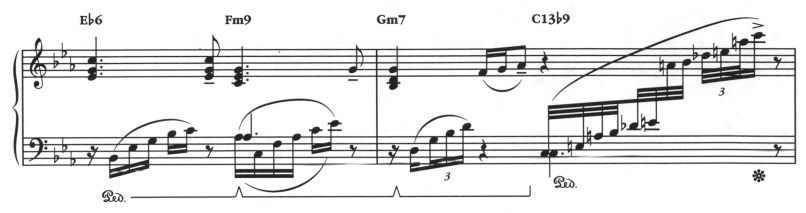

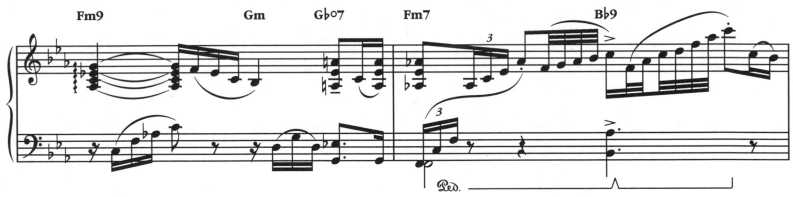

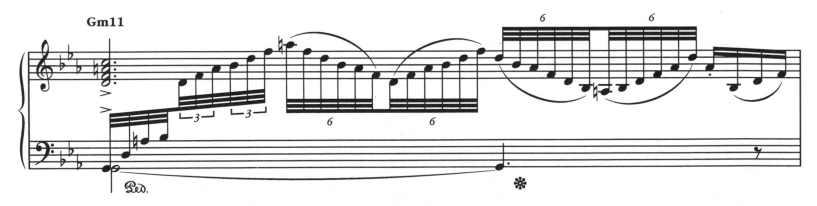

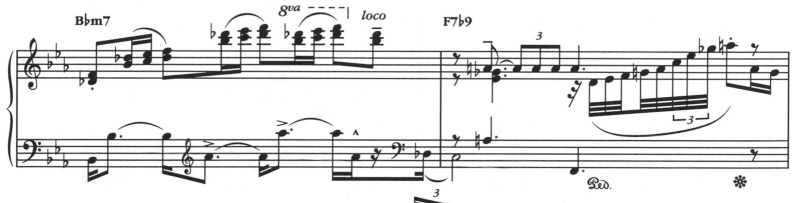

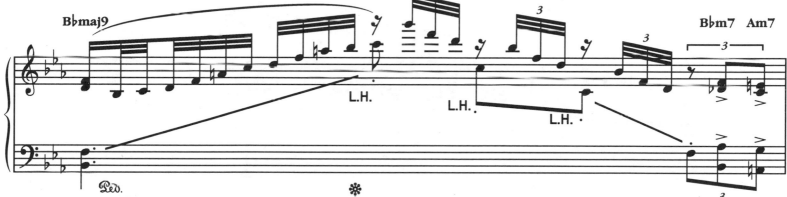

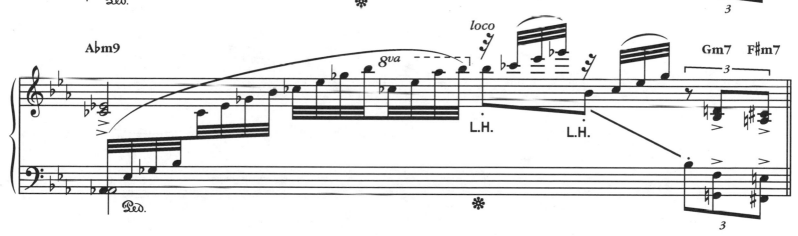

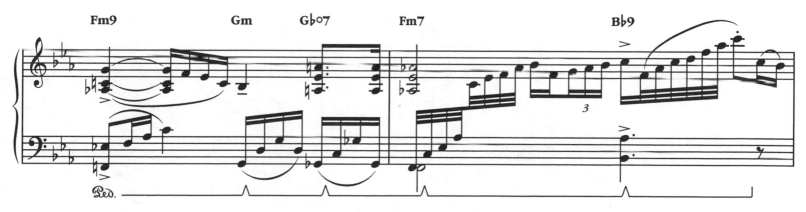

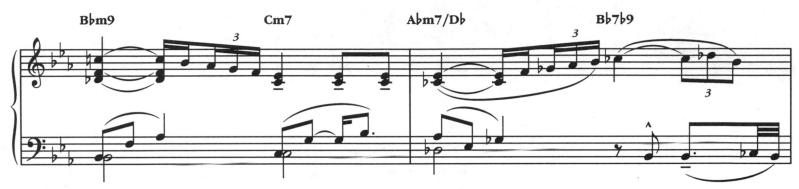

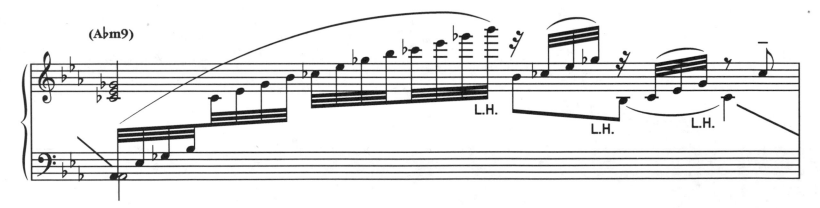

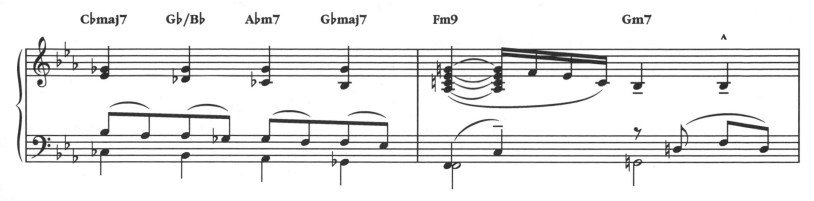

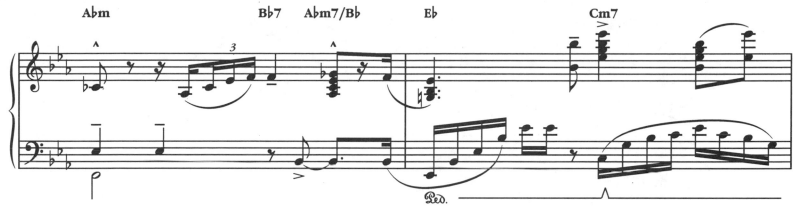

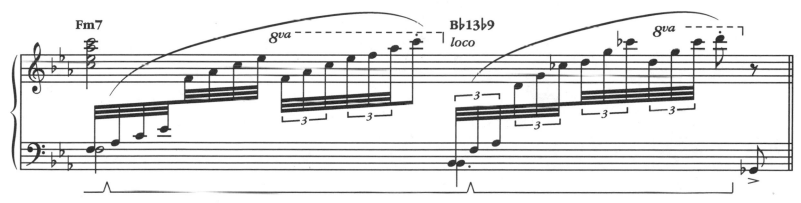

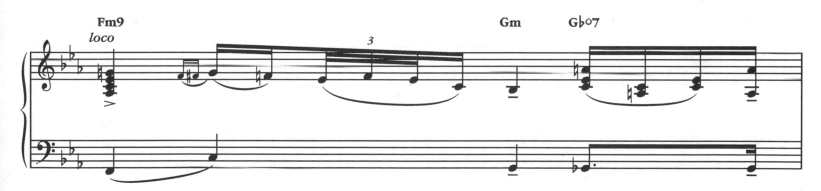

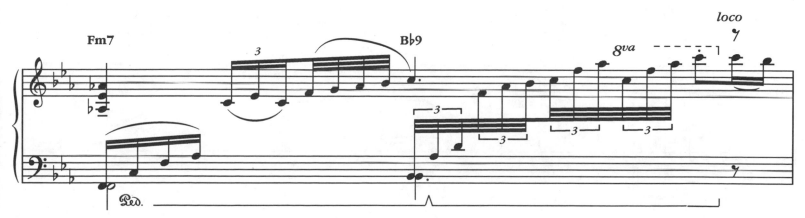

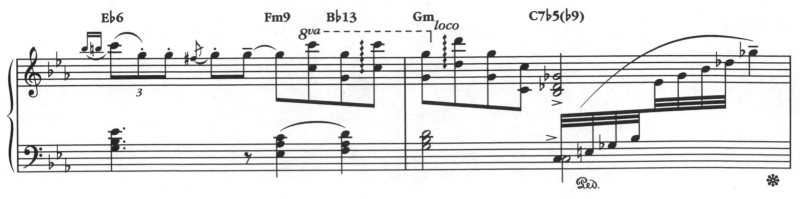

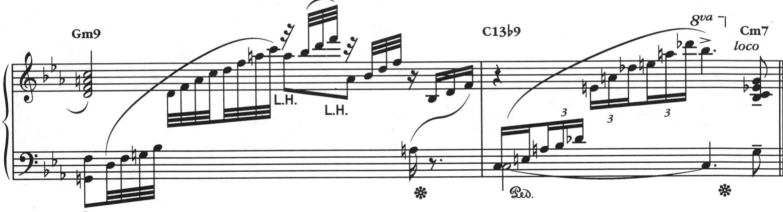

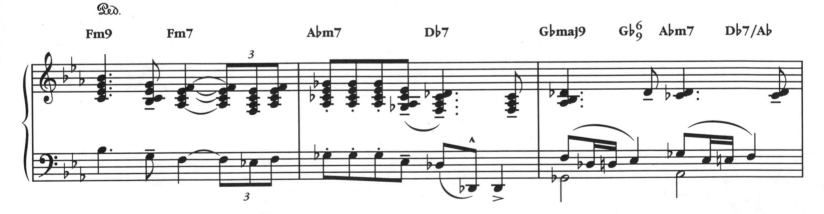

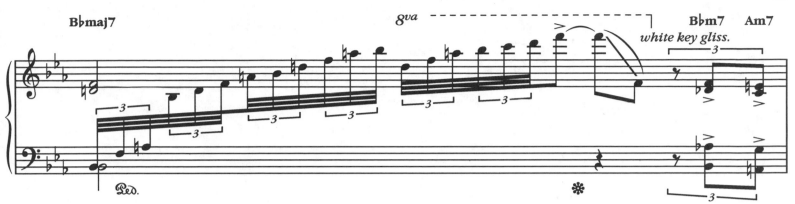

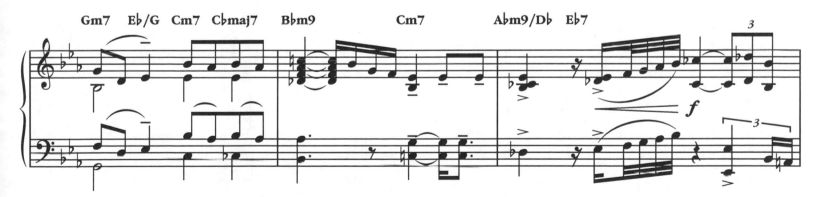

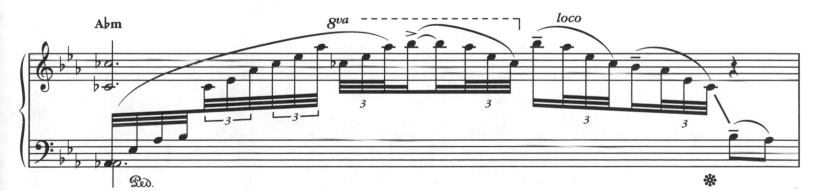

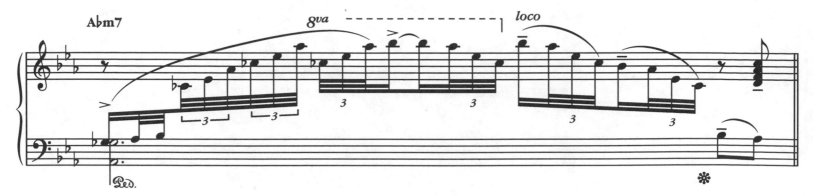

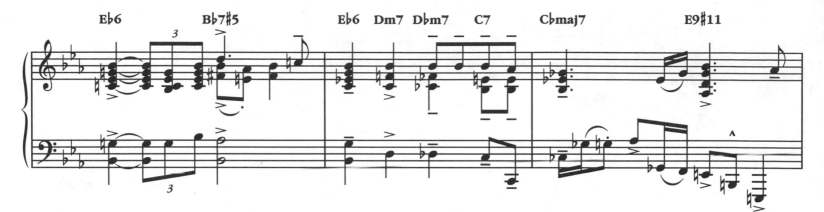

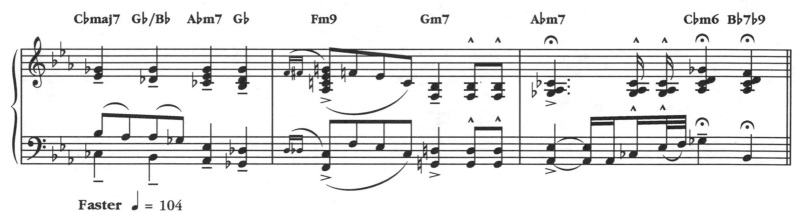

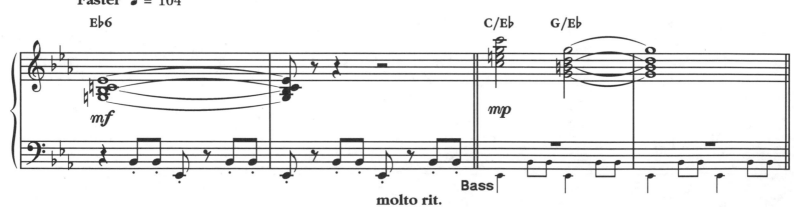

EASY LIVING

Theme from the Paramount Picture EASY LIVING

Words and Music by
LEO ROBIN and RALPH RAINGER

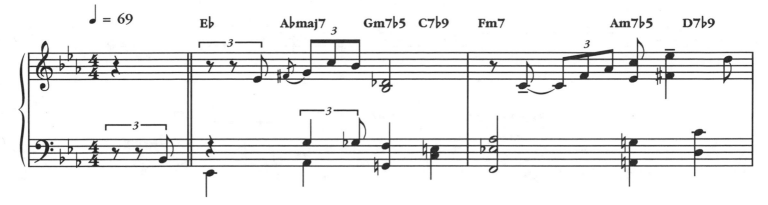

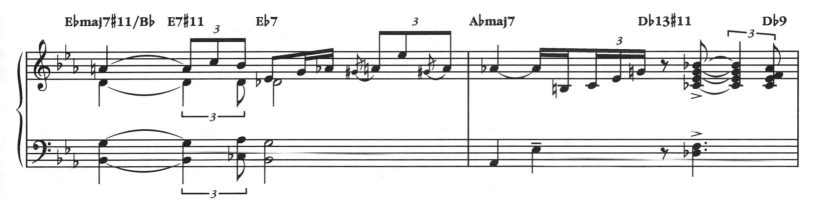

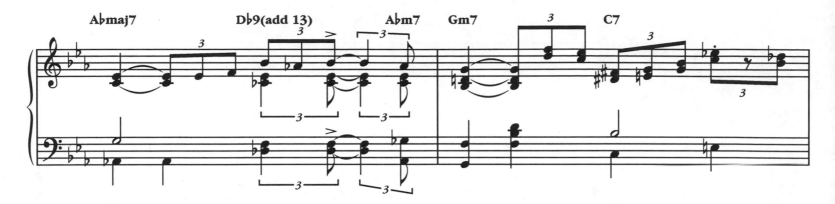

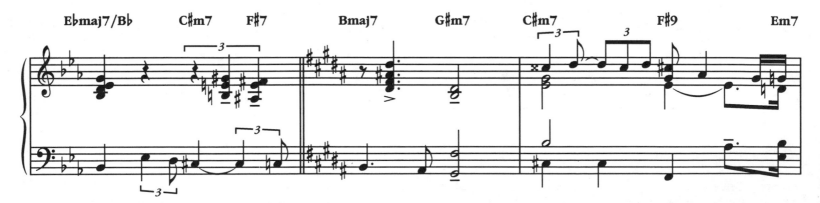

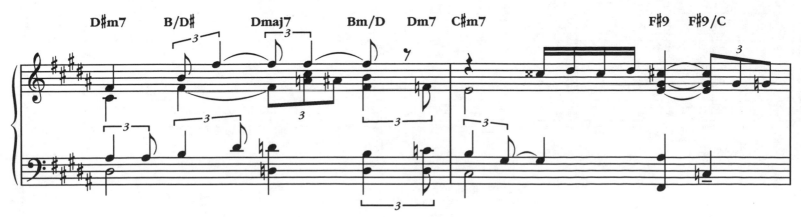

29

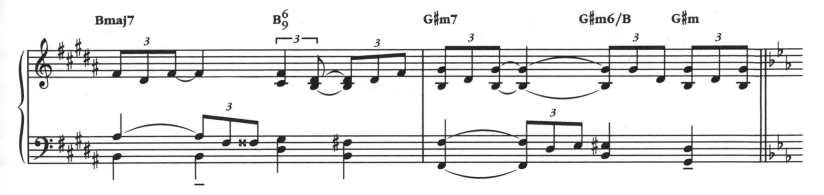

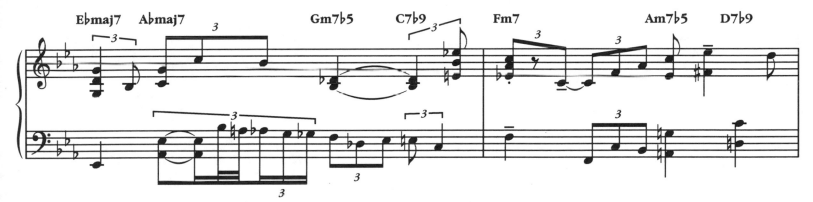

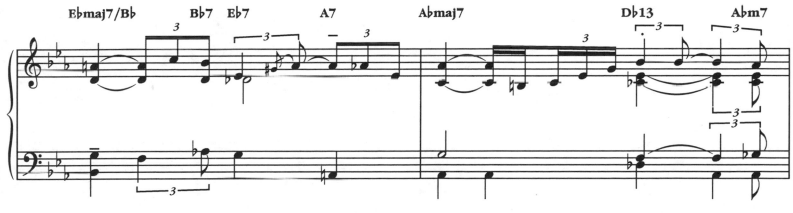

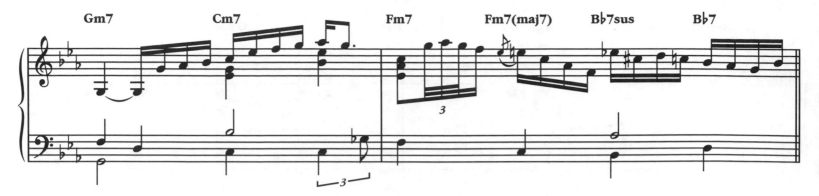

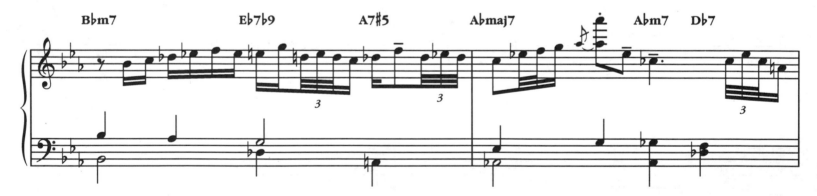

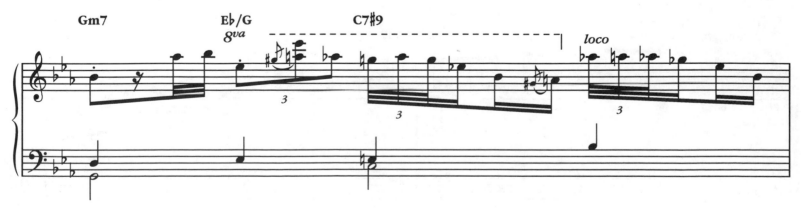

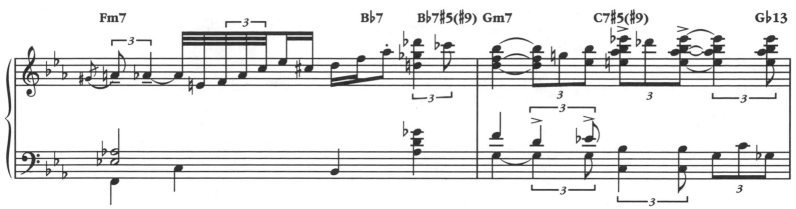

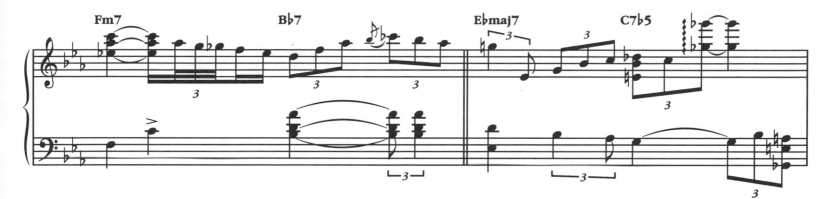

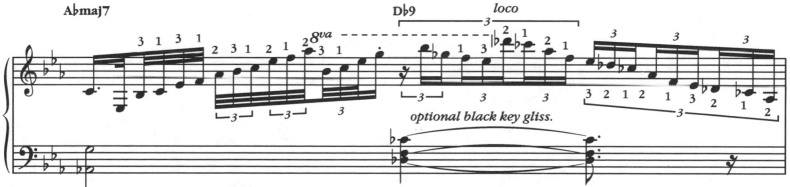

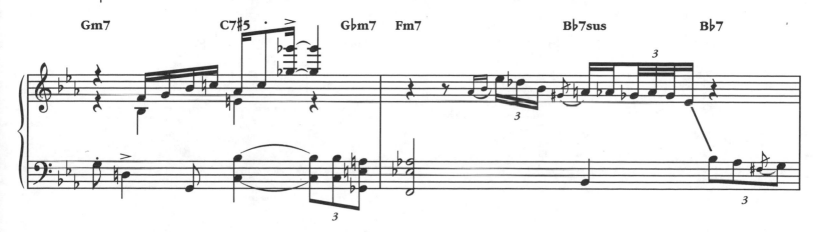

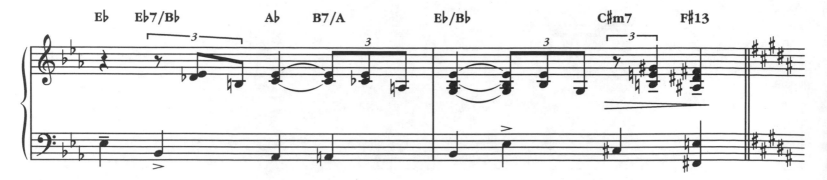

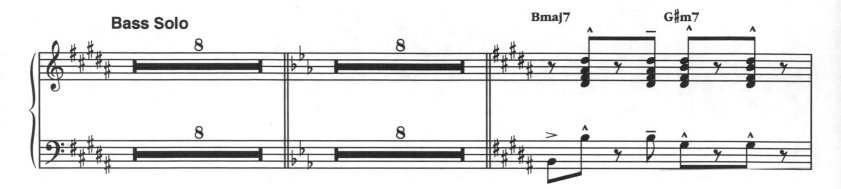

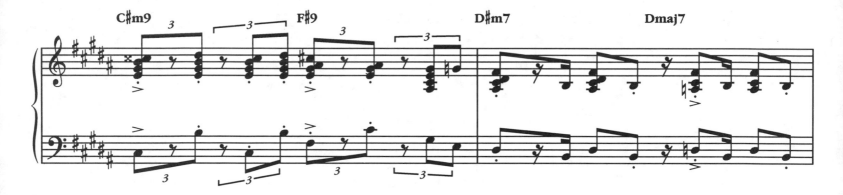

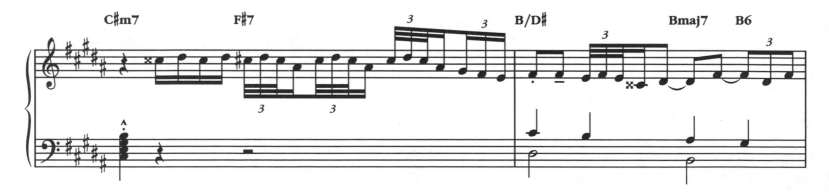

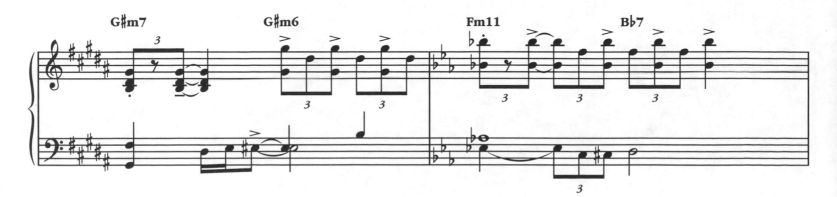

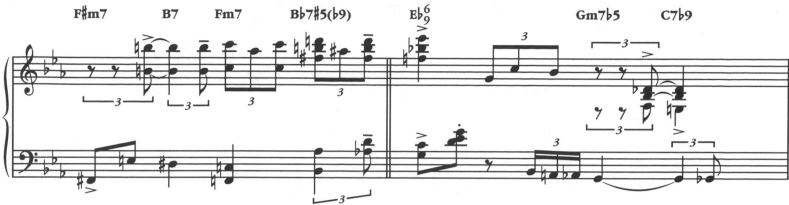

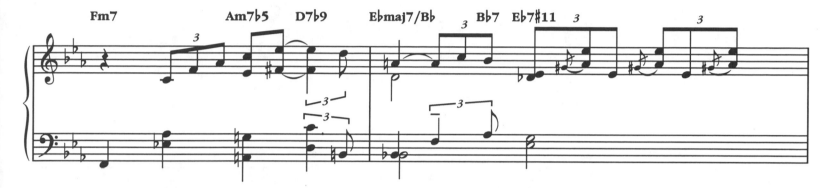

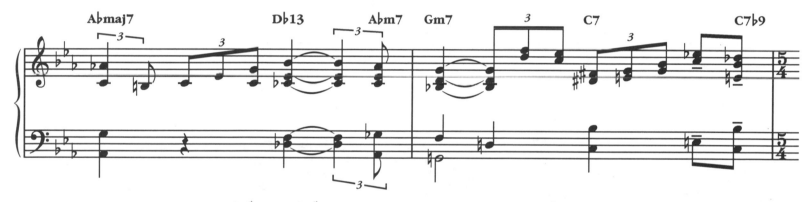

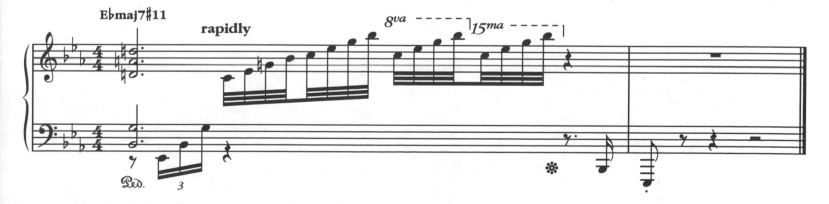

BODY AND SOUL

Words by EDWARD HEYMAN, ROBERT SOUR and FRANK EYTON
Music by JOHN GREEN

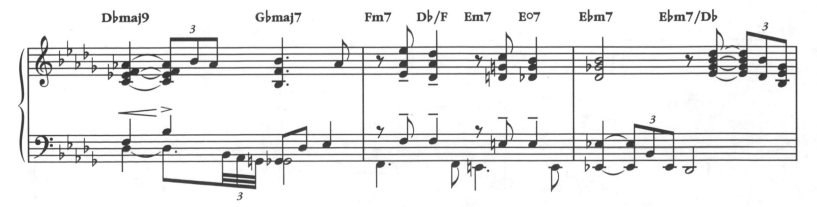

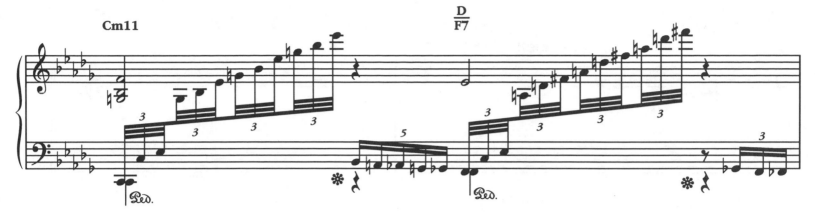

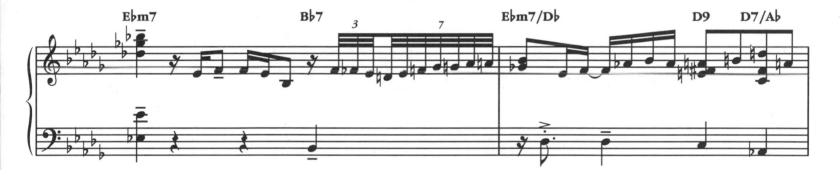

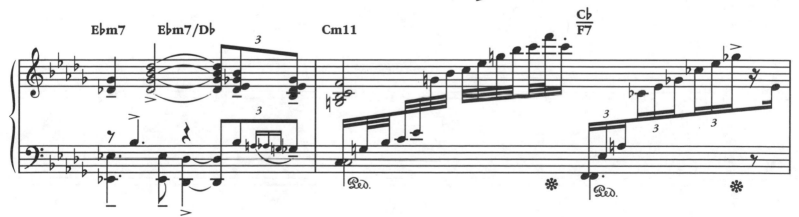

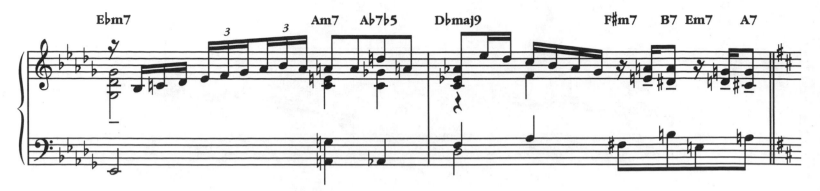

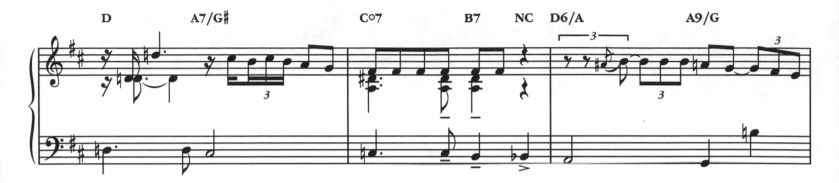

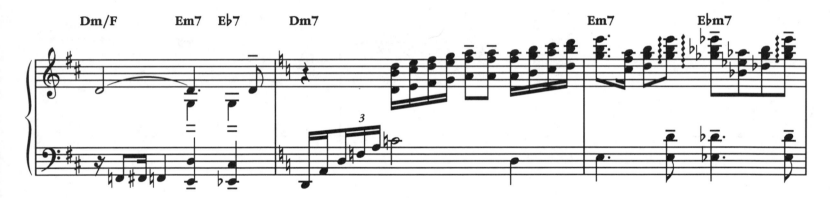

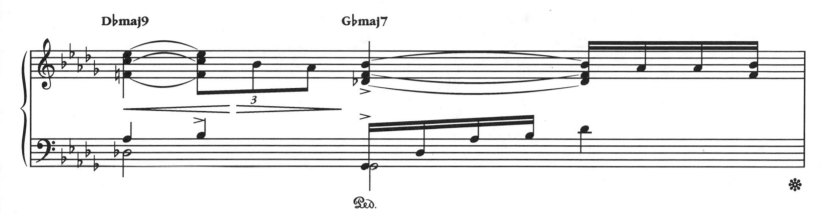

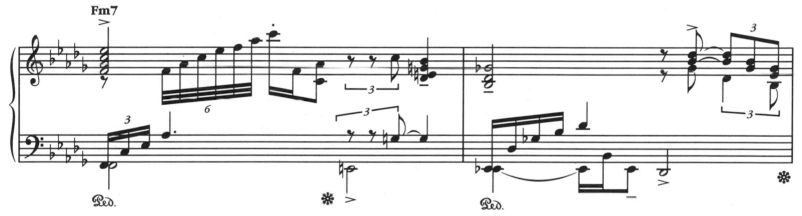

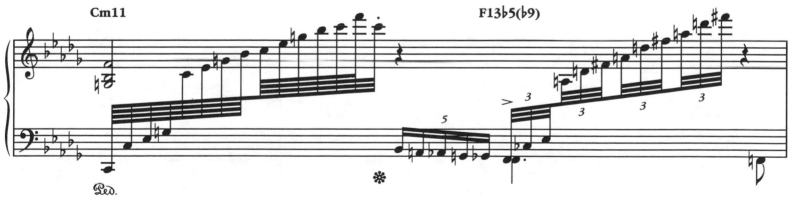

Bass Solo

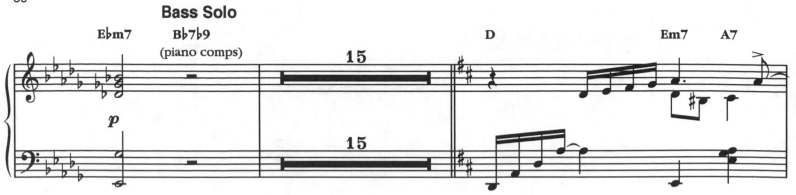

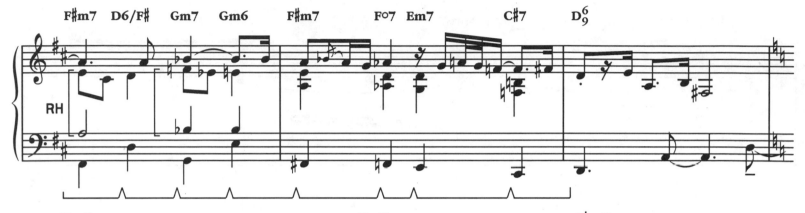

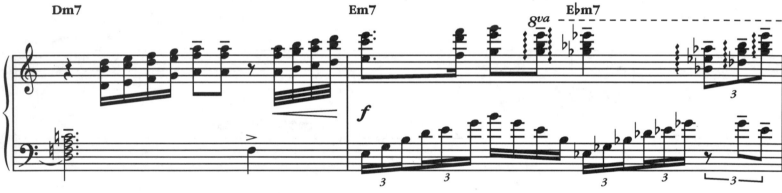

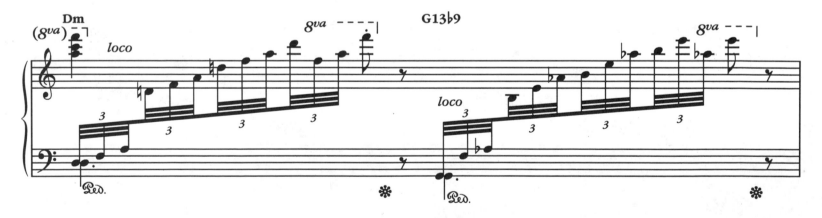

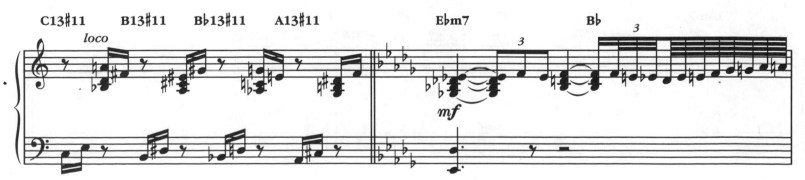

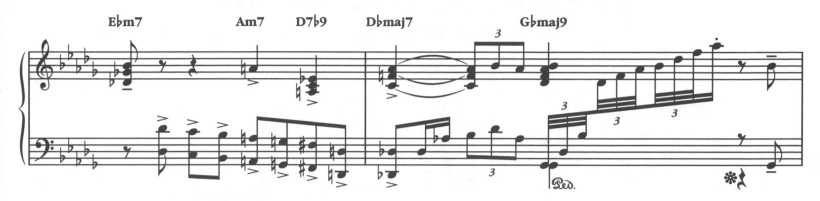

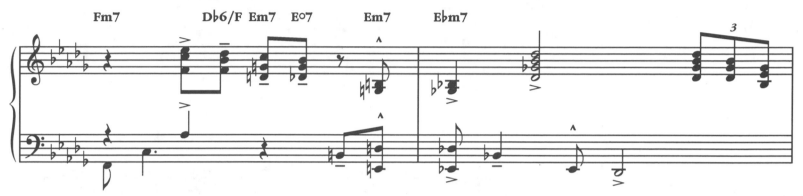

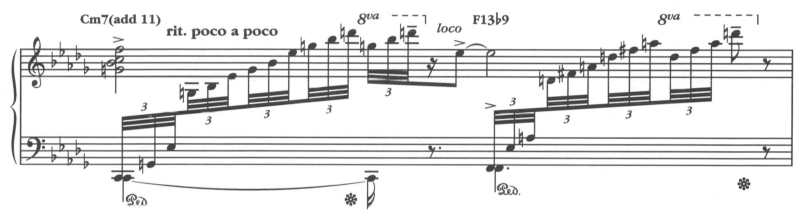

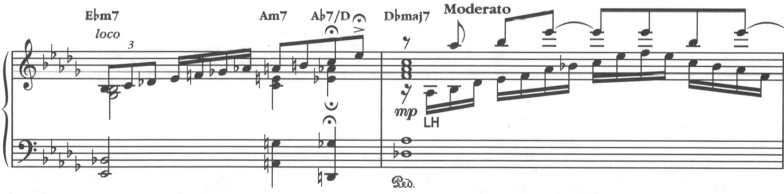

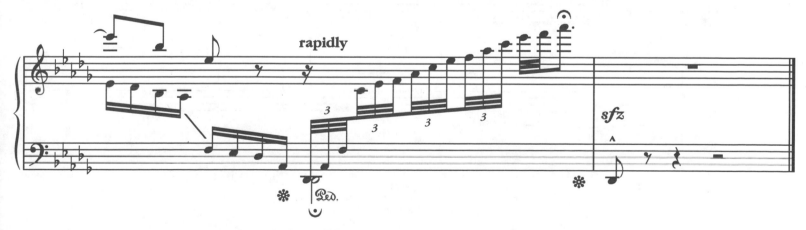

FLY ME TO THE MOON

(IN OTHER WORDS)

Words and Music by
BART HOWARD

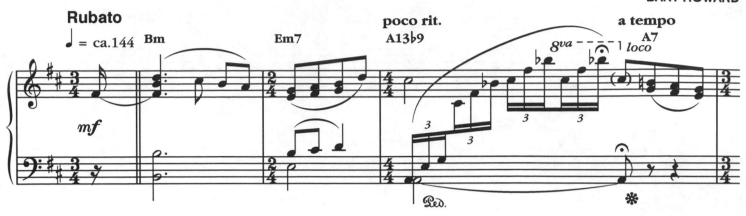

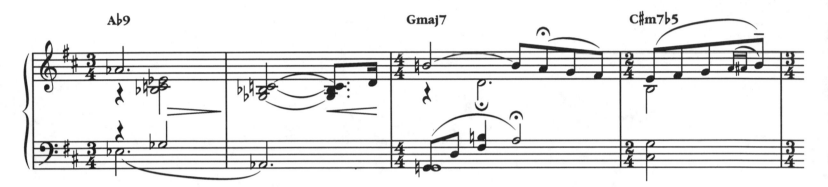

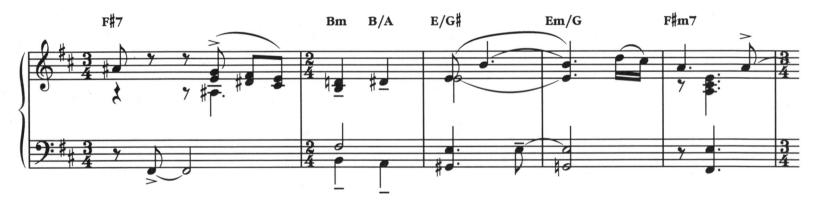

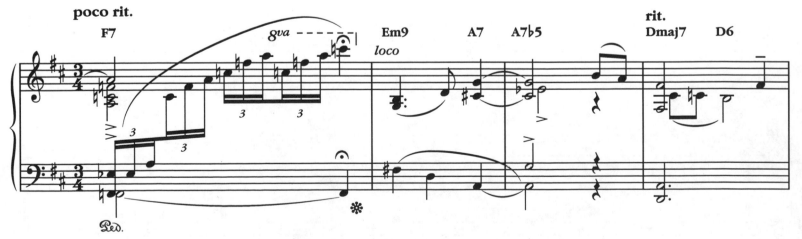

41

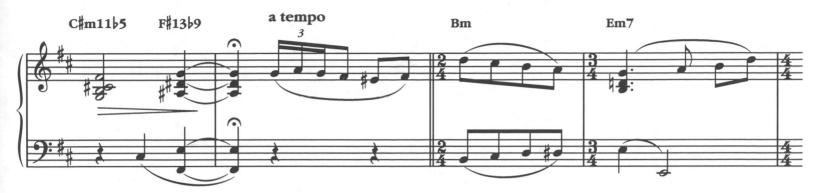

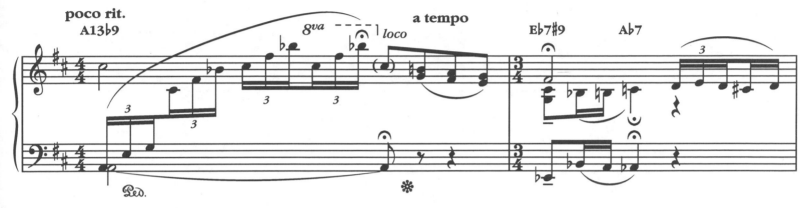

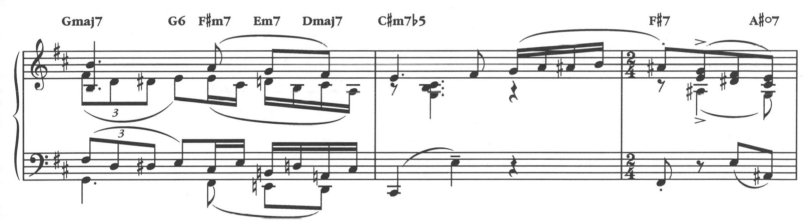

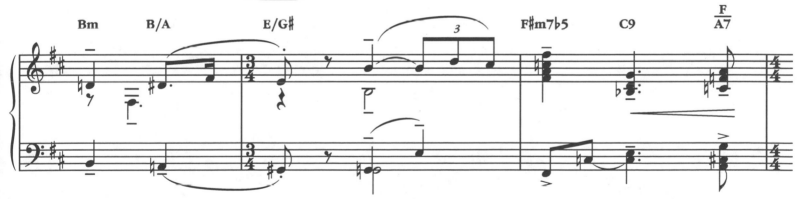

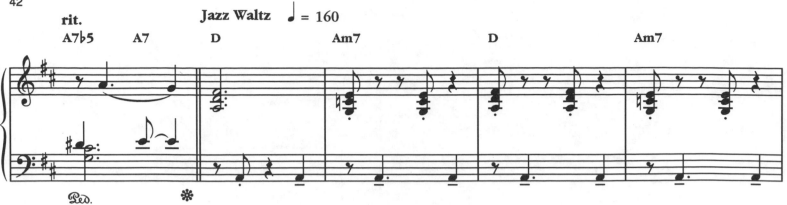

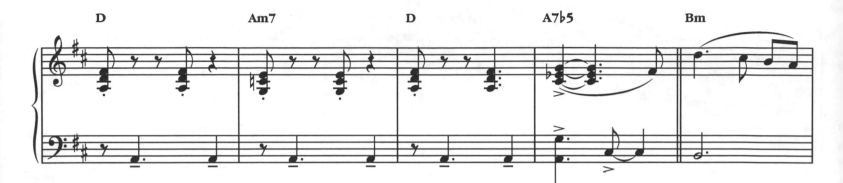

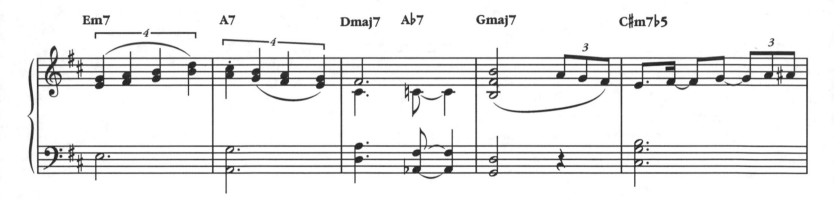

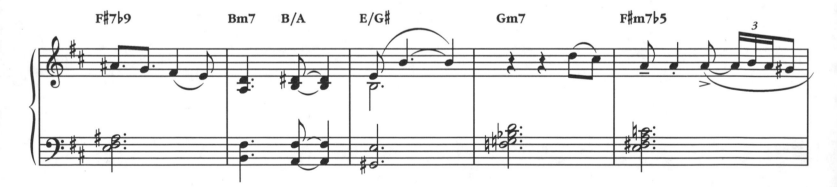

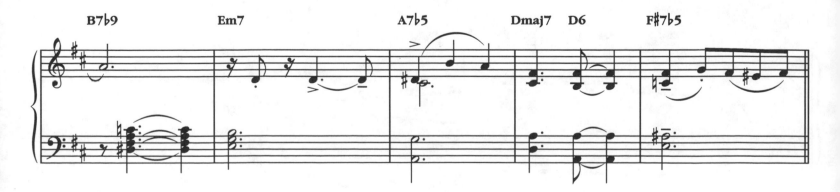

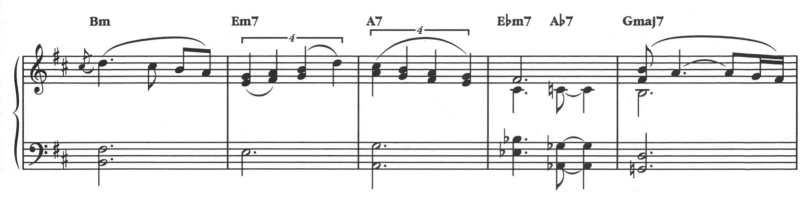

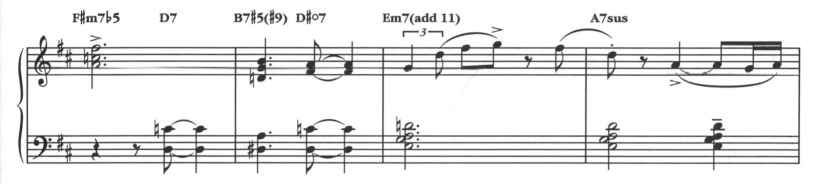

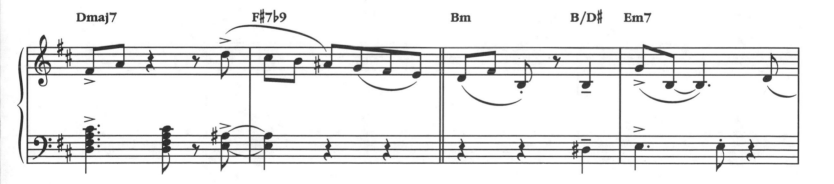

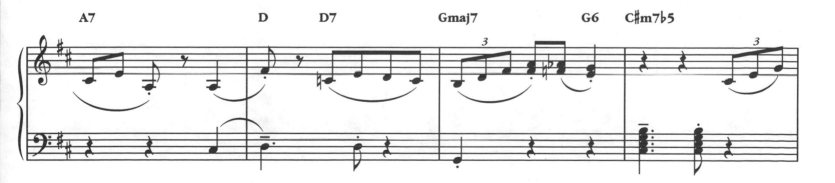

44

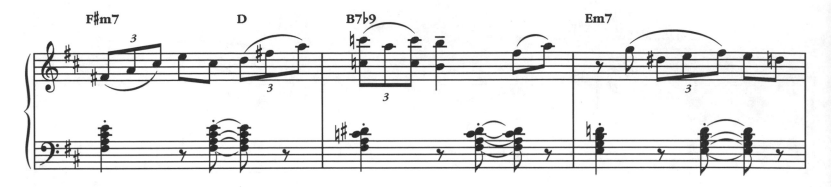

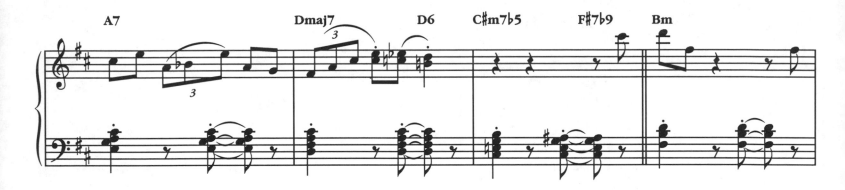

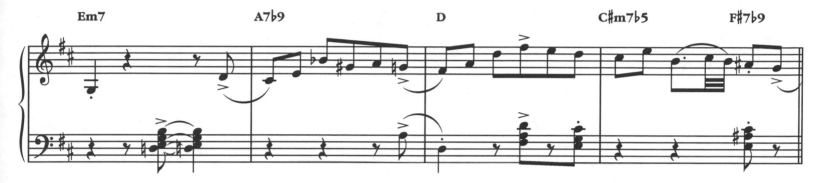

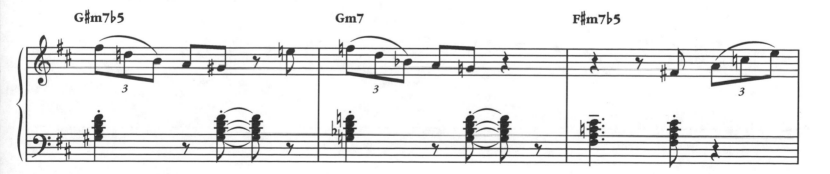

46

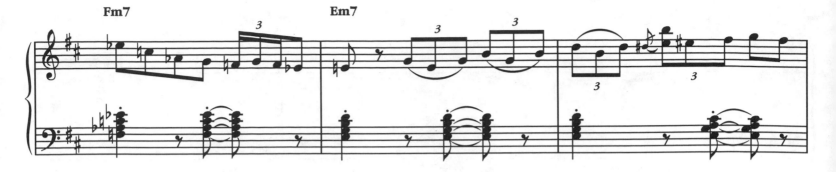

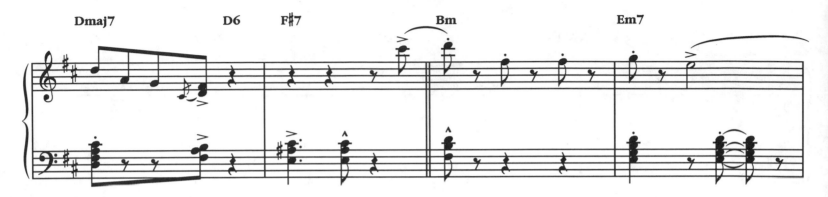

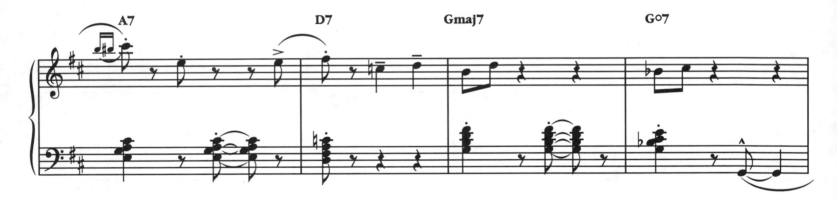

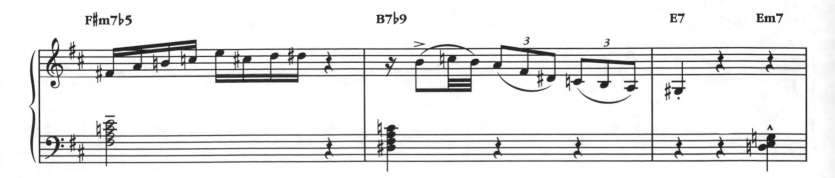

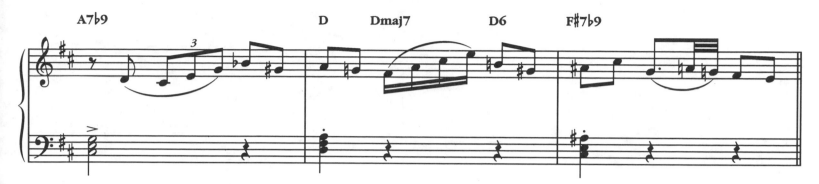

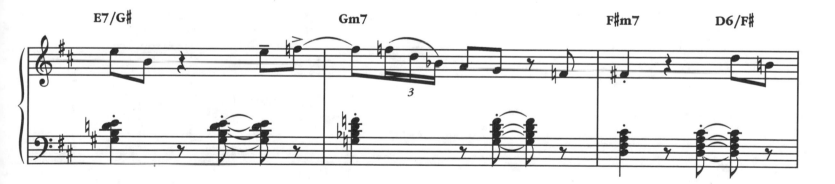

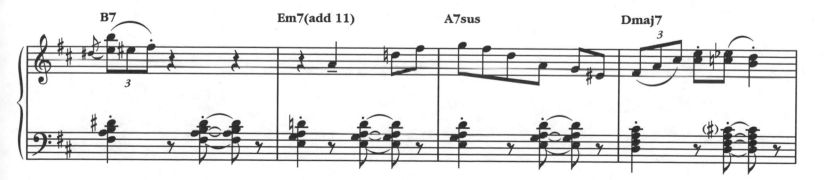

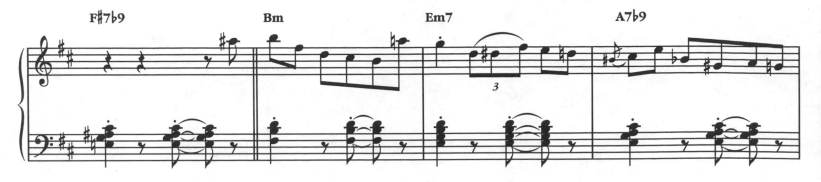

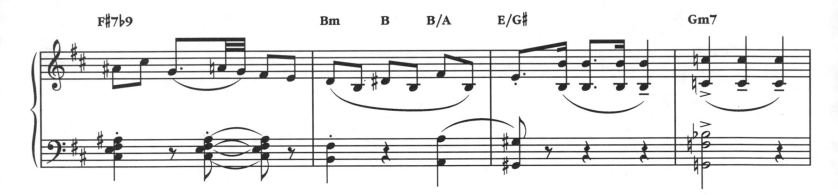

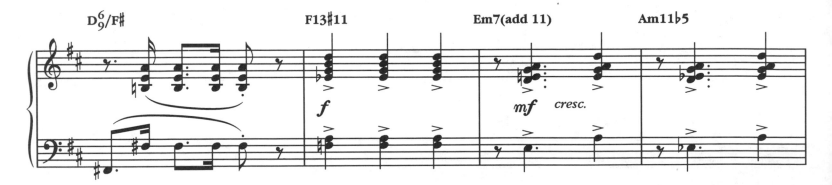

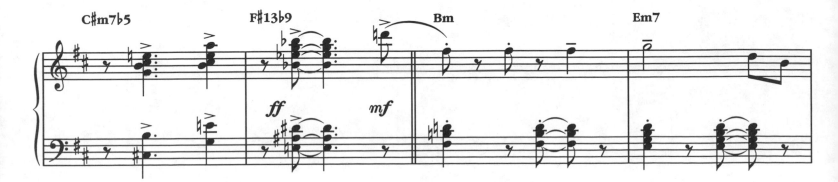

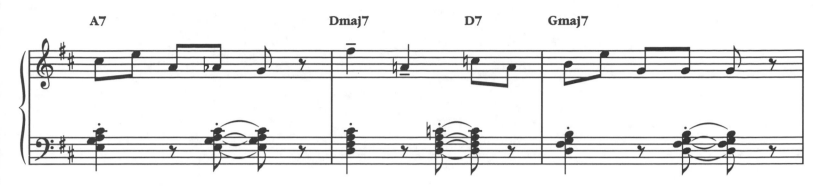

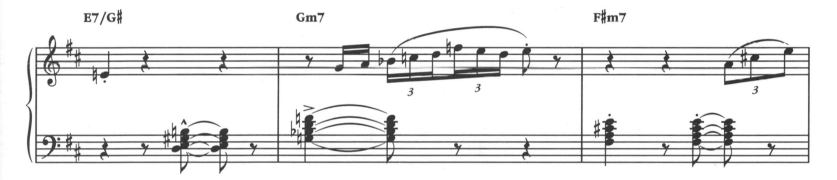

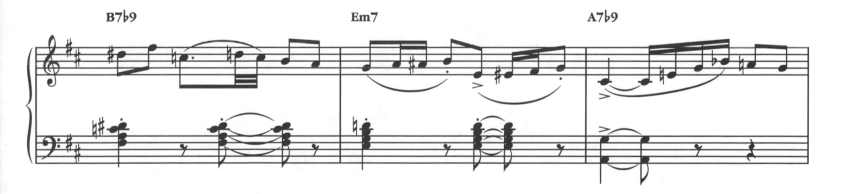

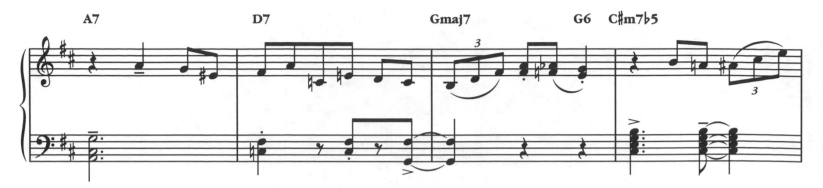

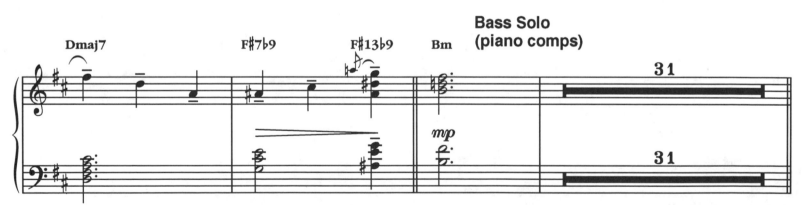

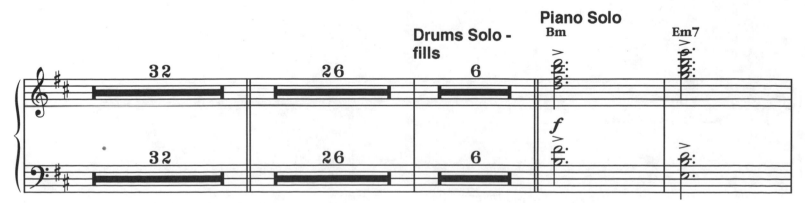

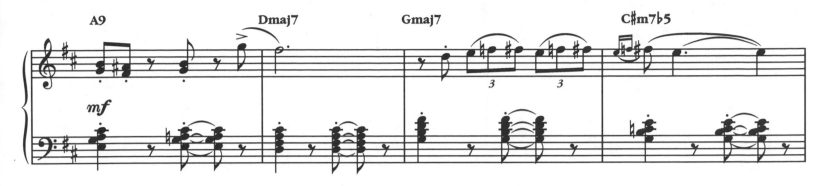

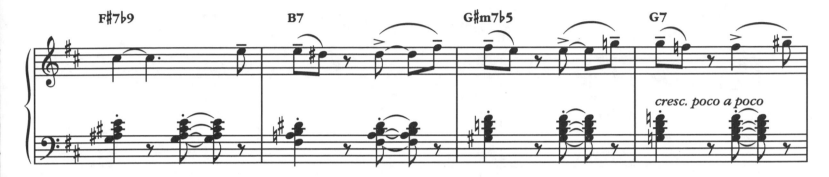

Drums Solo

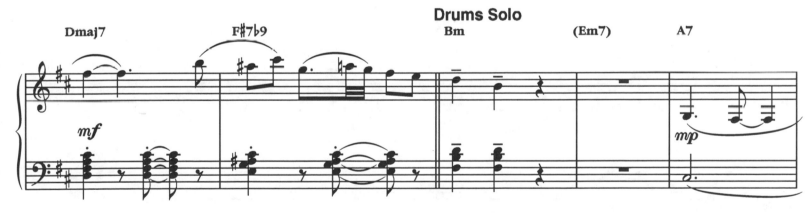

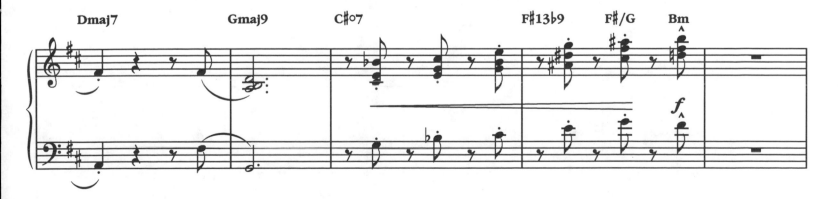

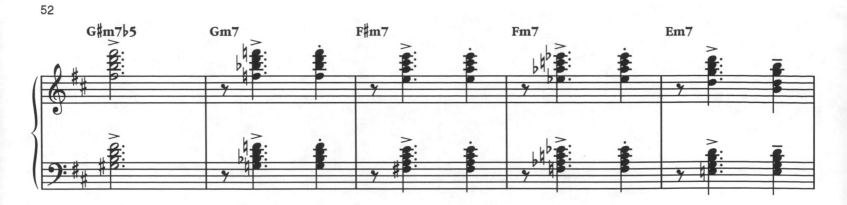

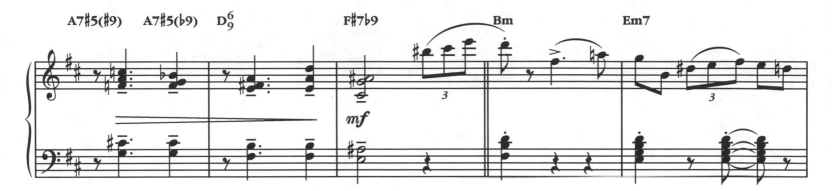

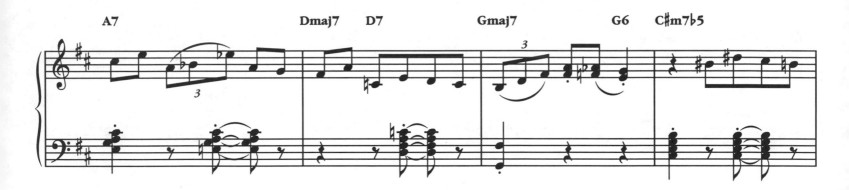

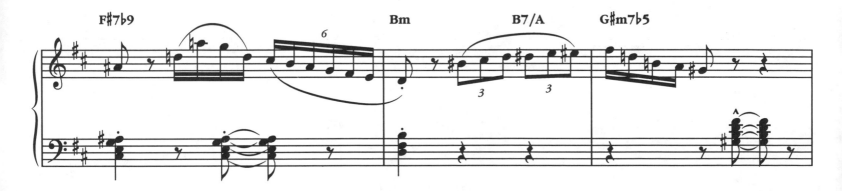

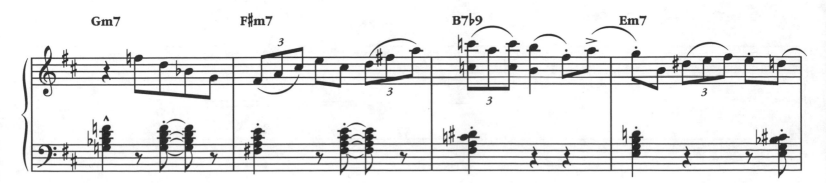

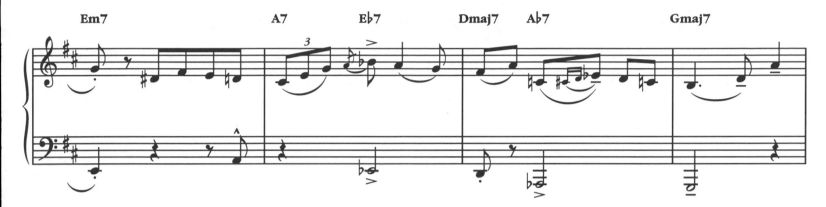

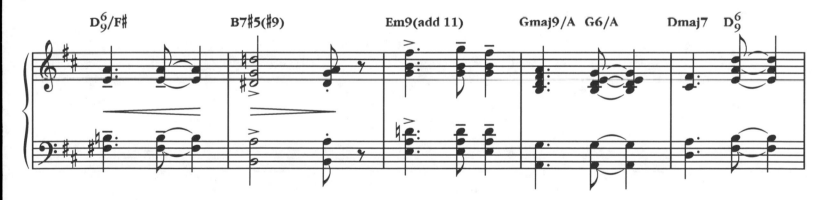

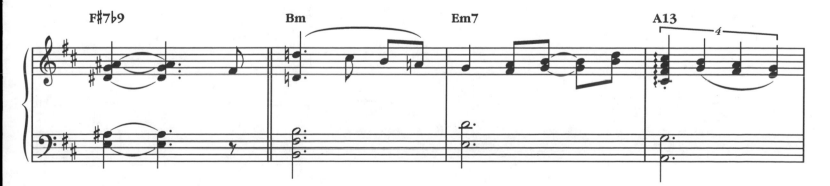

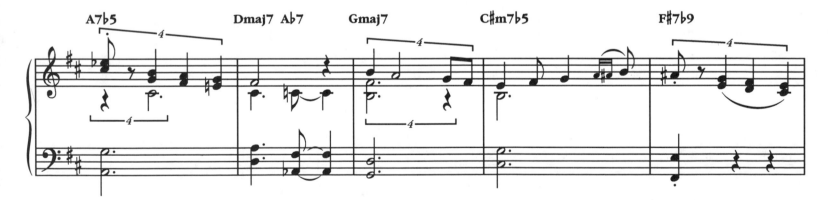

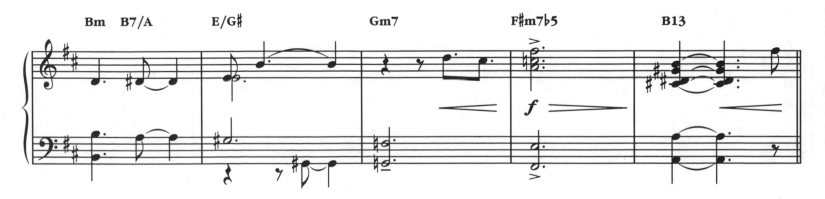

I REMEMBER YOU

from the Paramount Picture THE FLEET'S IN

Words by JOHNNY MERCER
Music by VICTOR SCHERTZINGER

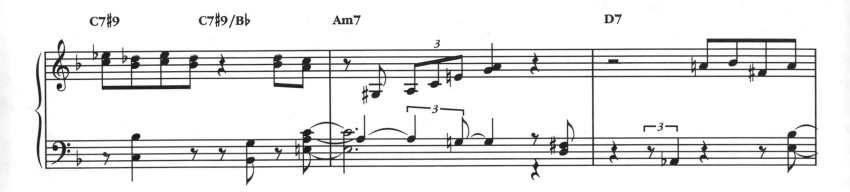

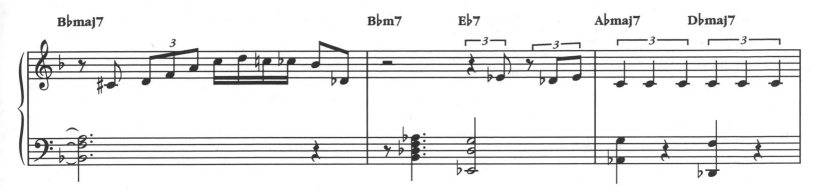

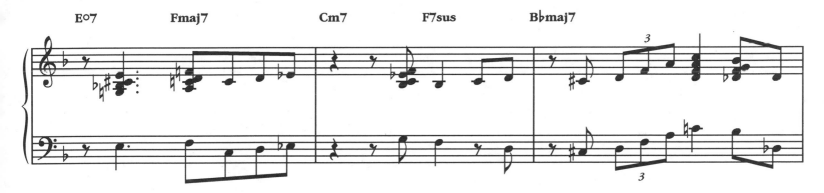

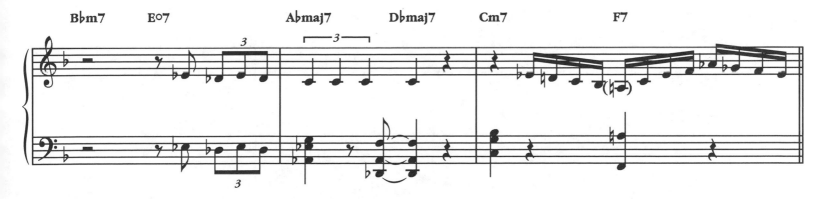

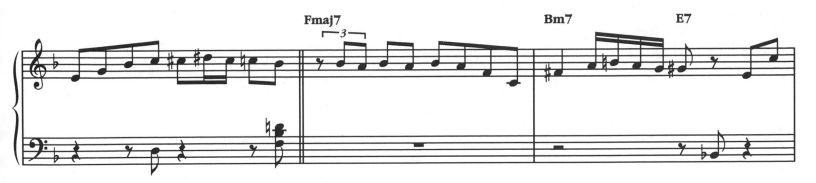

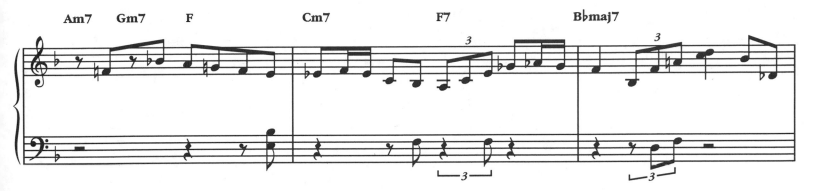

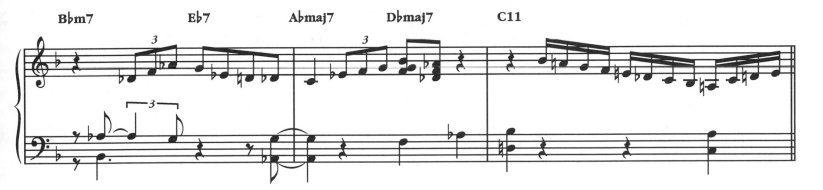

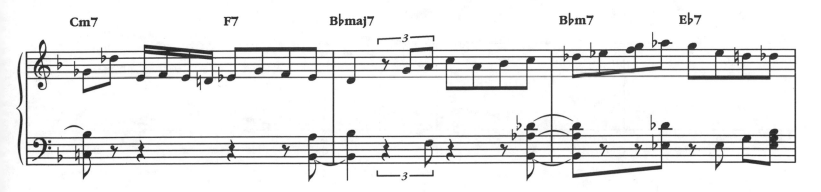

59

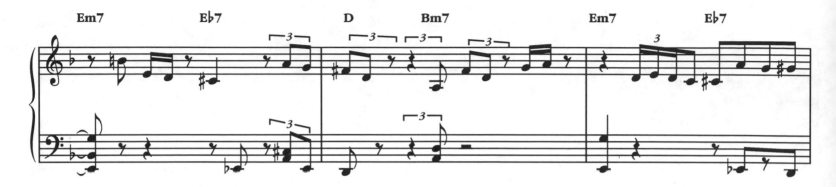

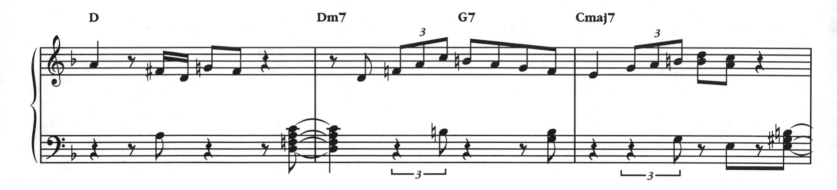

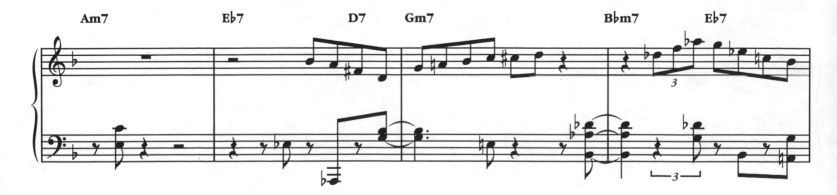

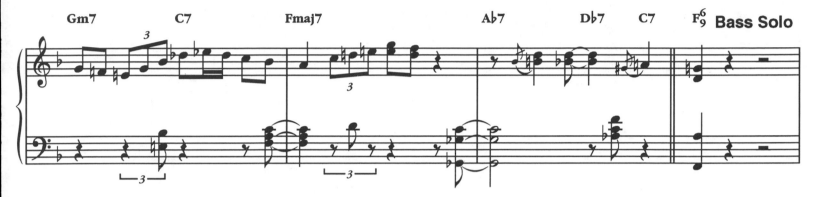

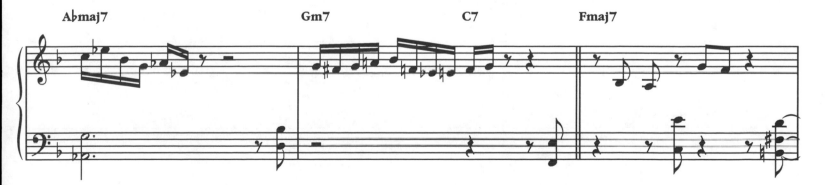

62

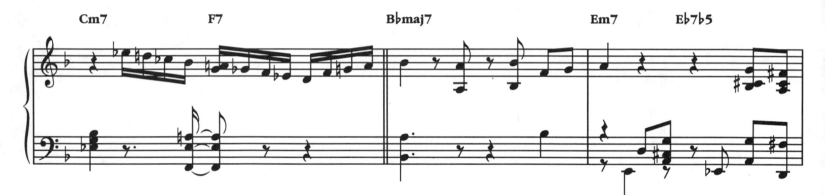

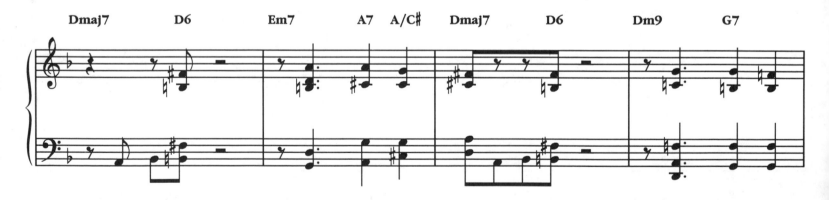

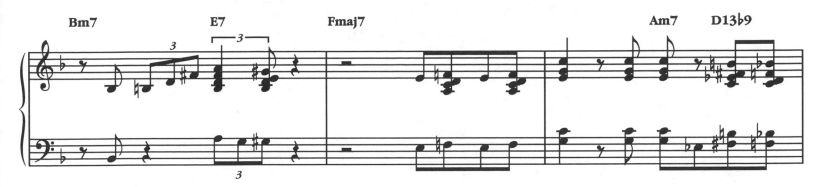

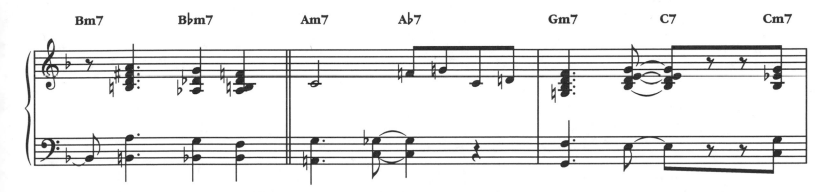

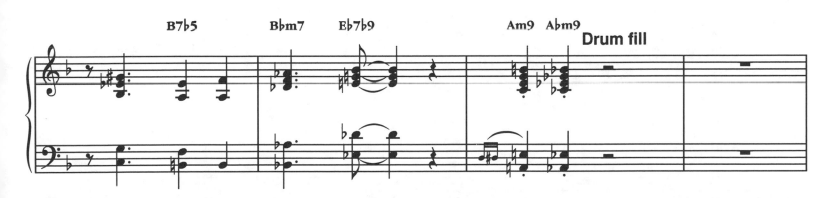

STELLA BY STARLIGHT

from the Paramount Picture THE UNINVITED

Words by NED WASHINGTON
Music by VICTOR YOUNG

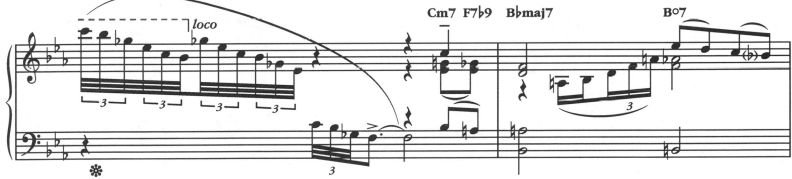

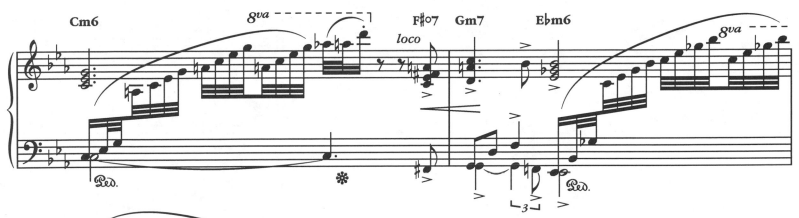

66

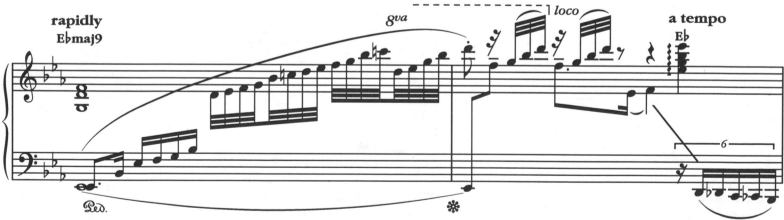

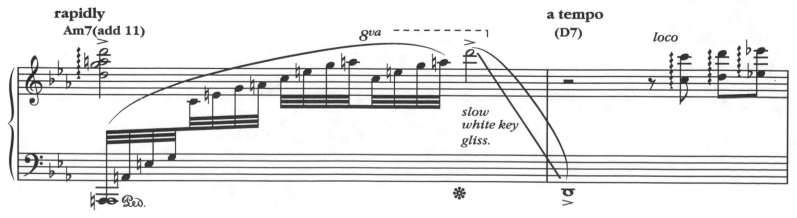

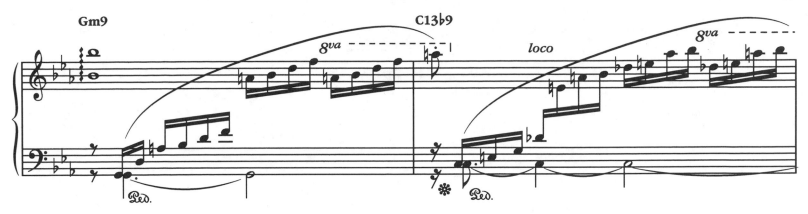

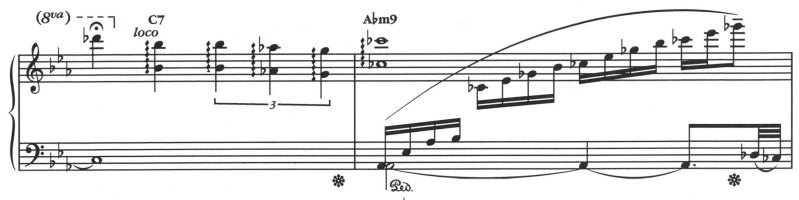

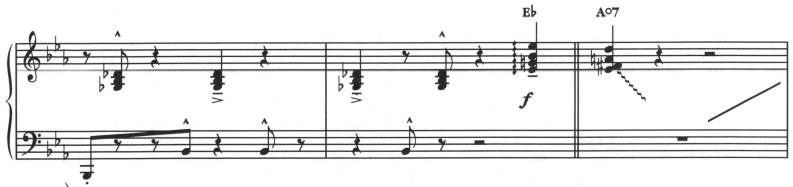

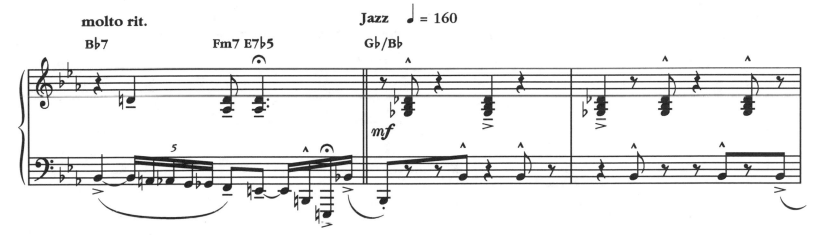

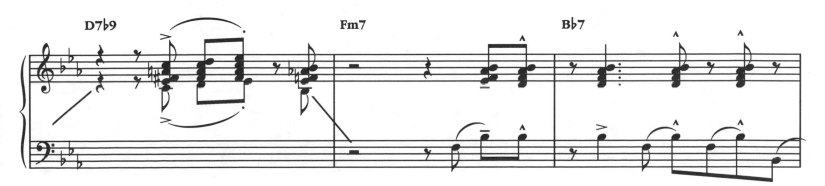

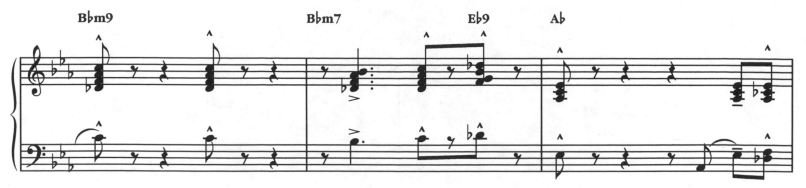

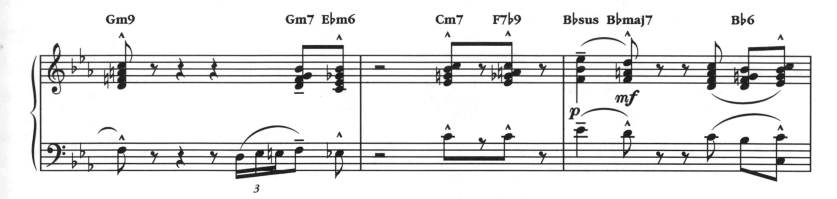

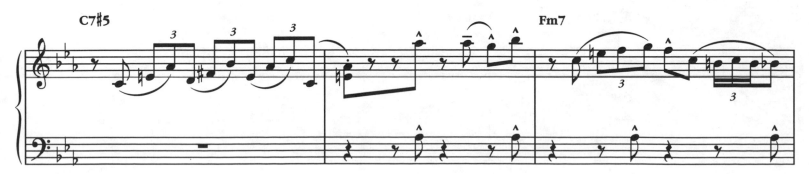

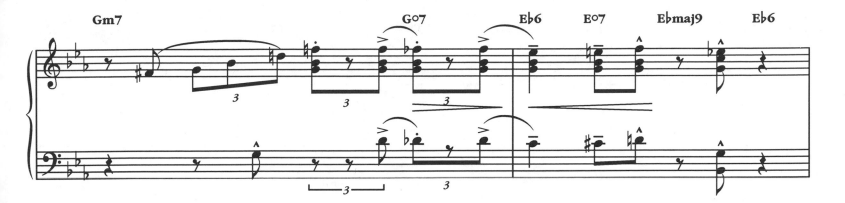

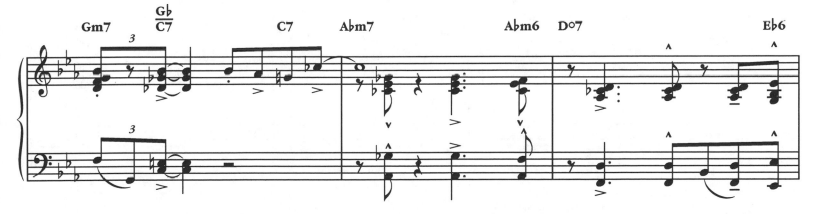

70

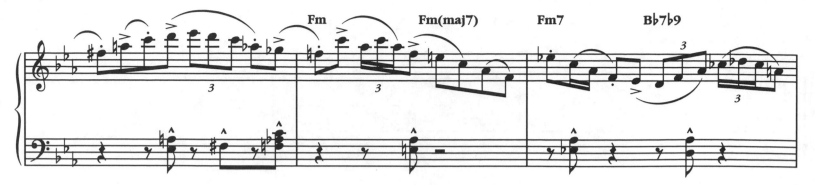

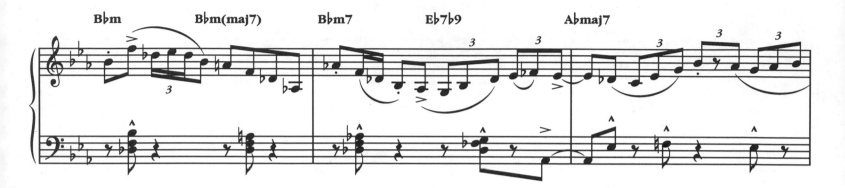

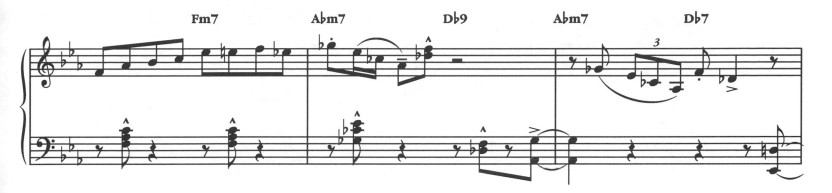

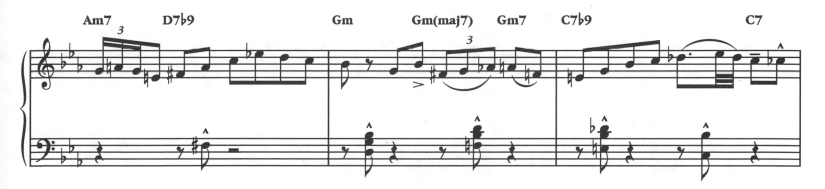

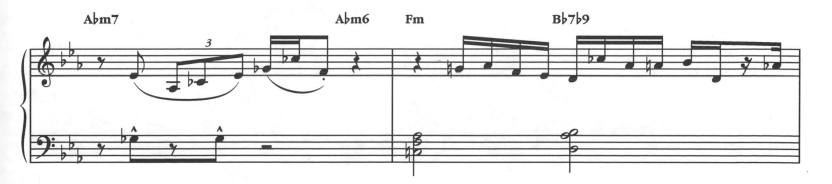

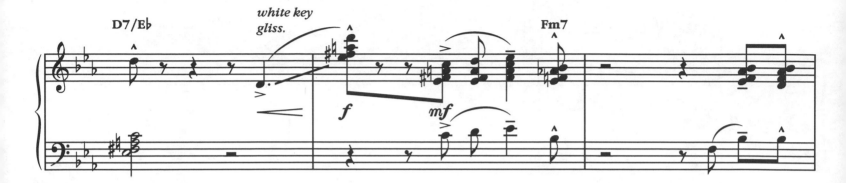

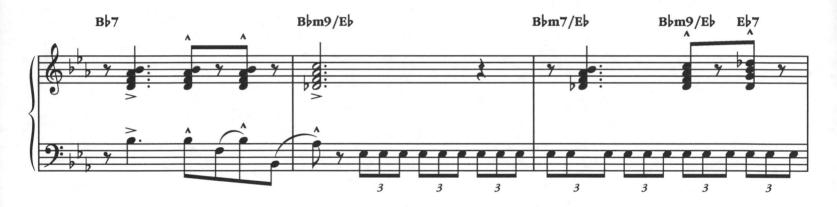

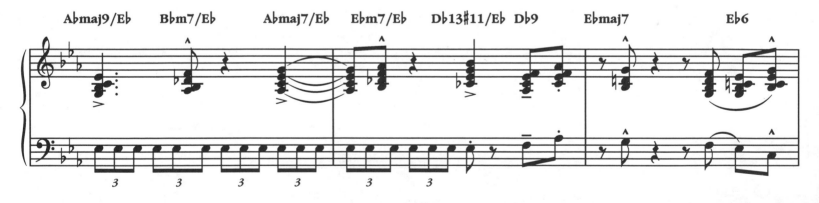

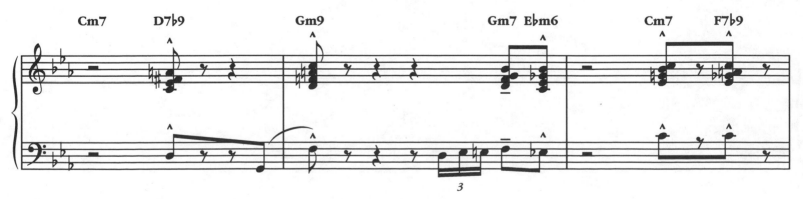

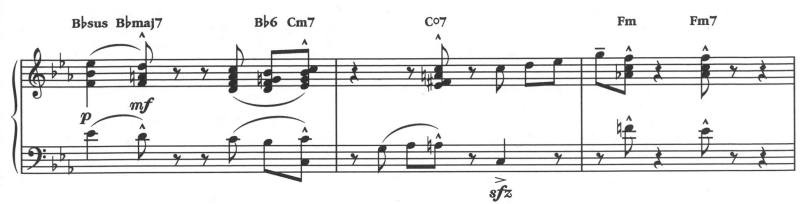

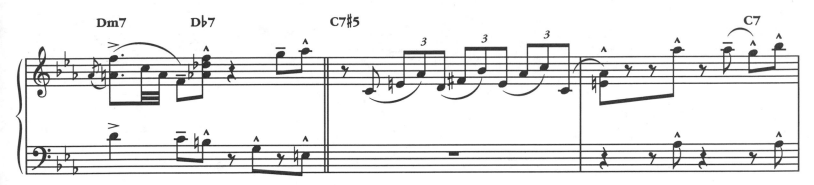

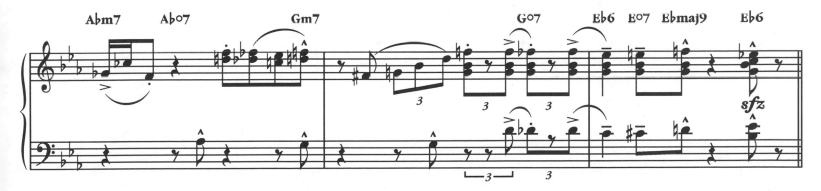

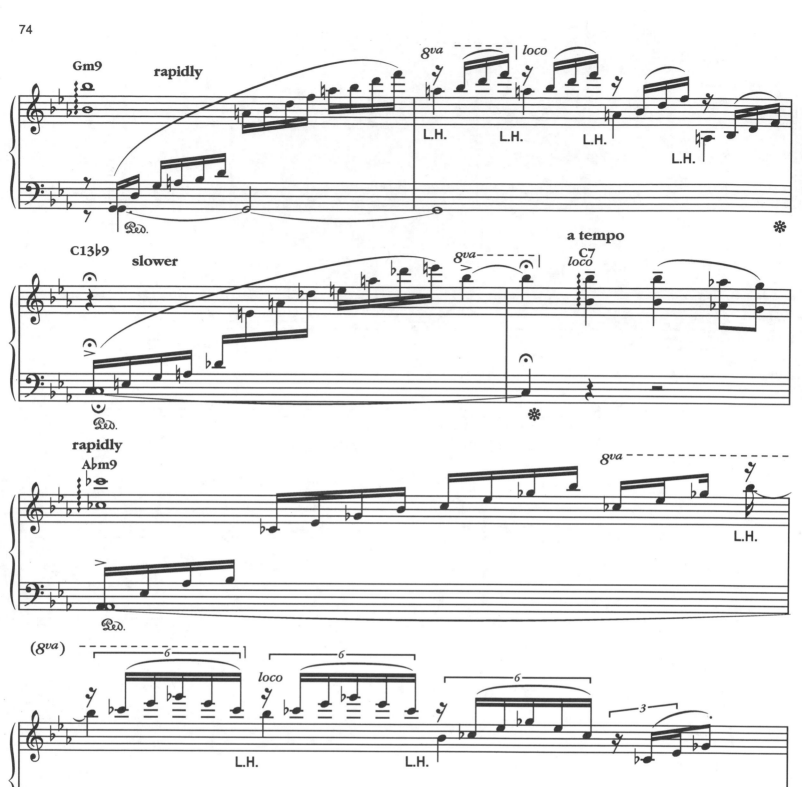

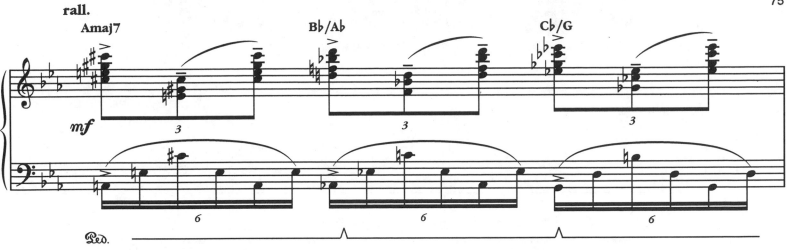

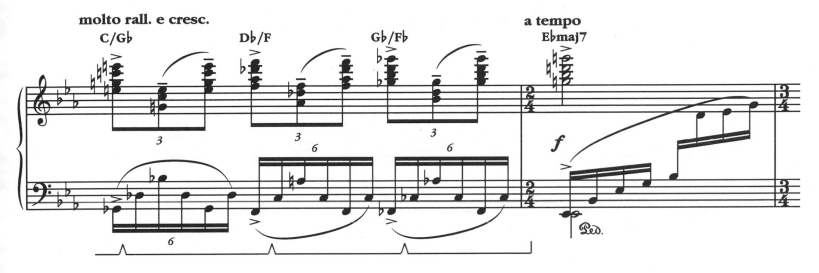

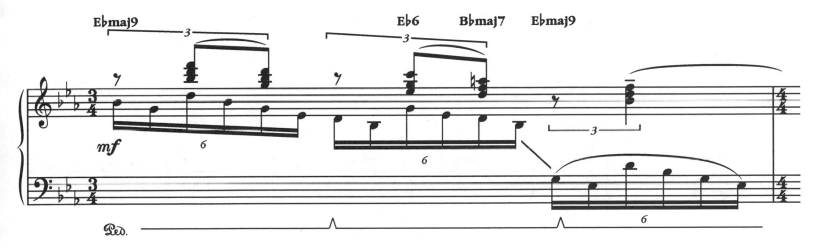

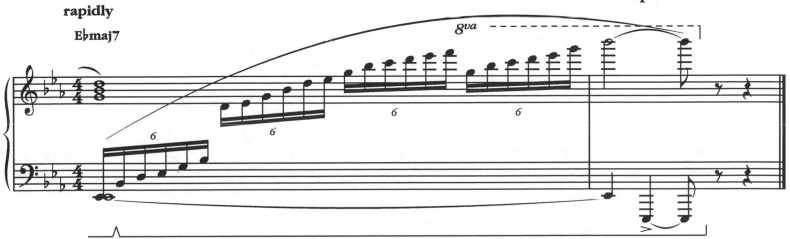

LOVER, COME BACK TO ME

from THE NEW MOON

Lyrics by OSCAR HAMMERSTEIN II
Music by SIGMUND ROMBERG

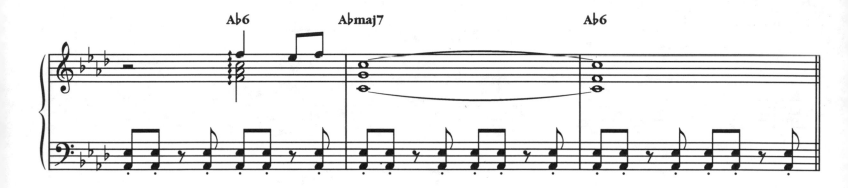

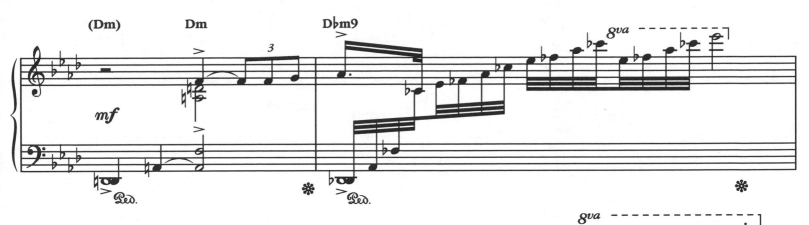

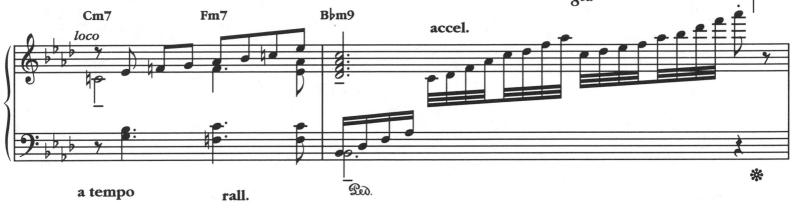

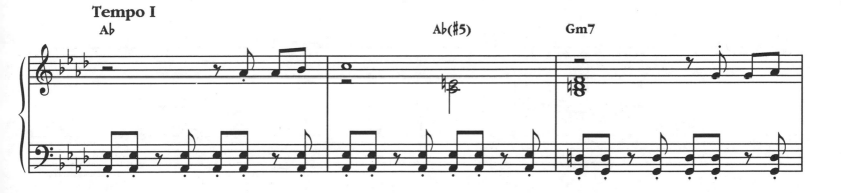

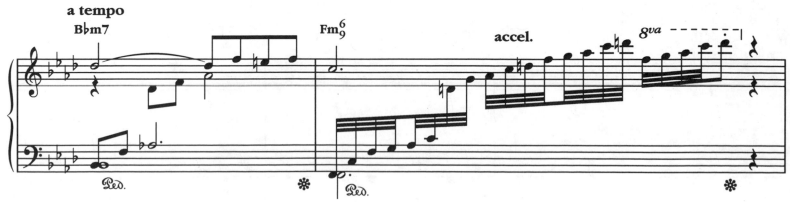

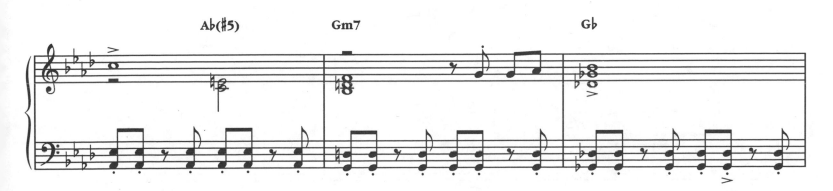

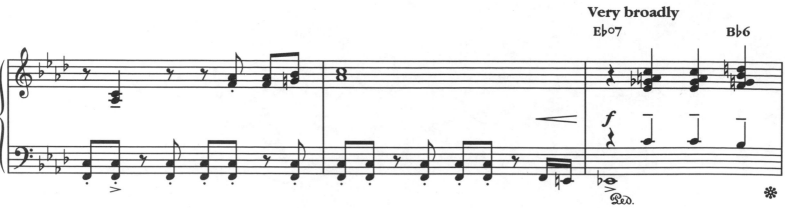

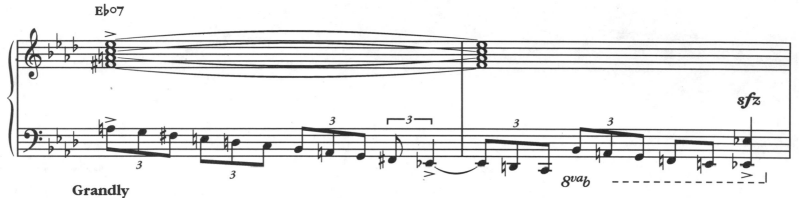

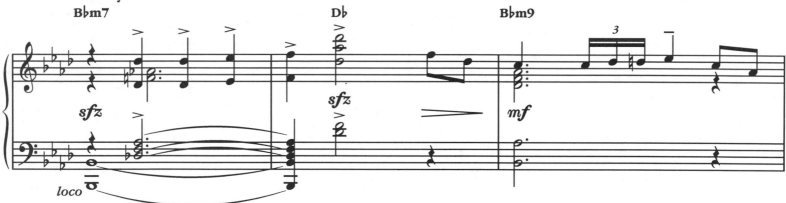

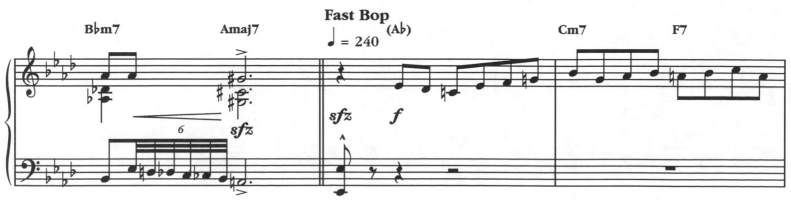

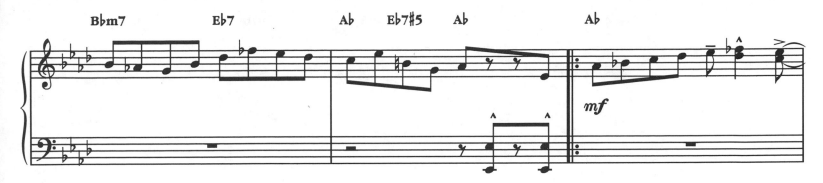

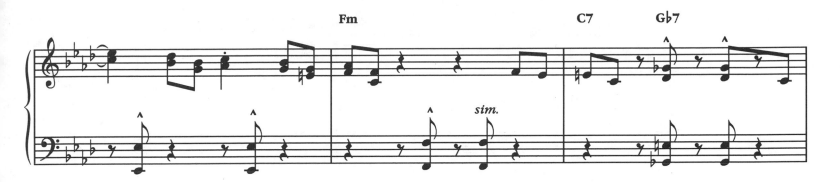

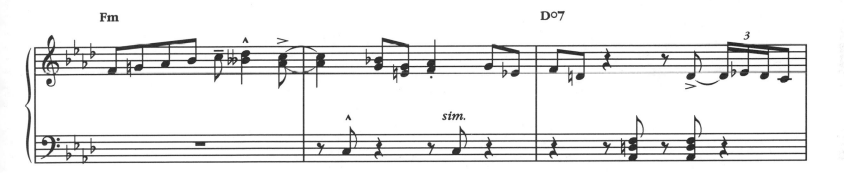

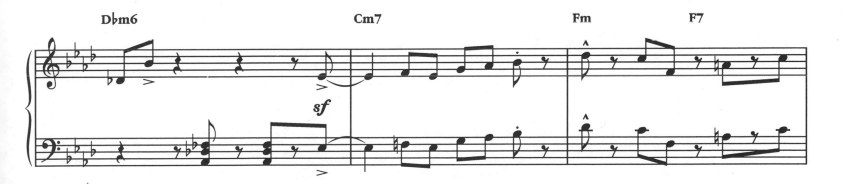

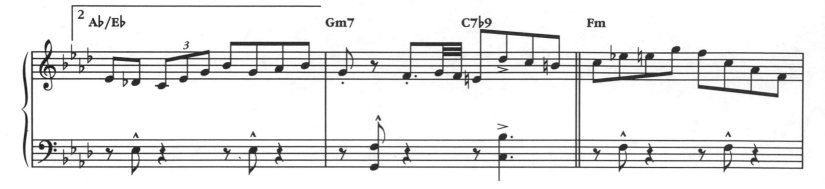

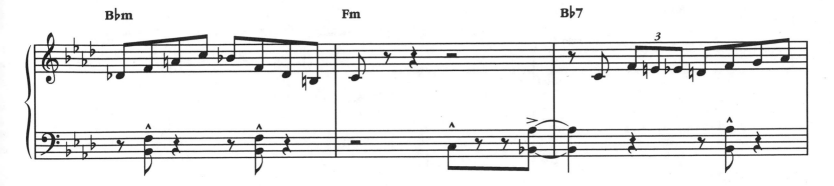

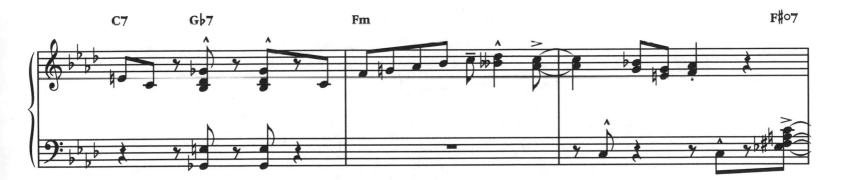

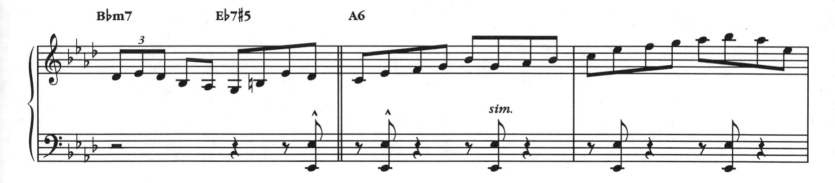

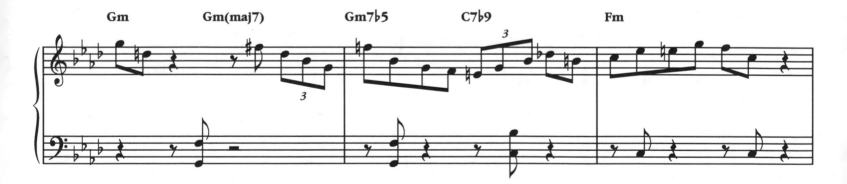

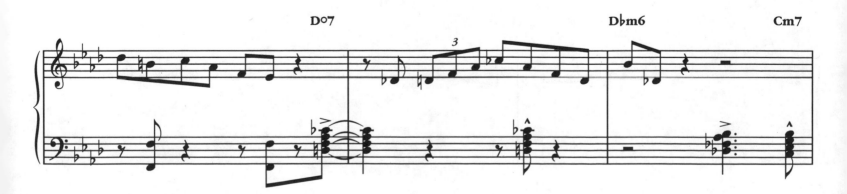

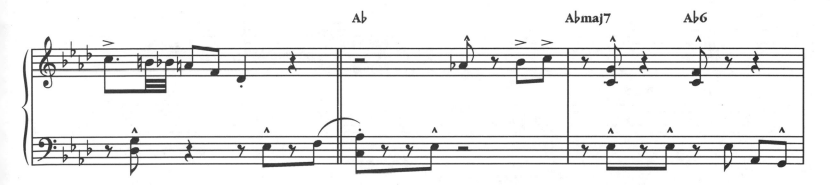

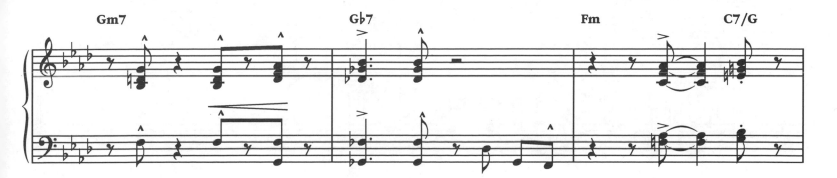

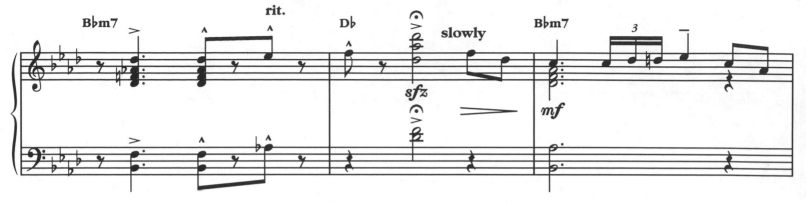

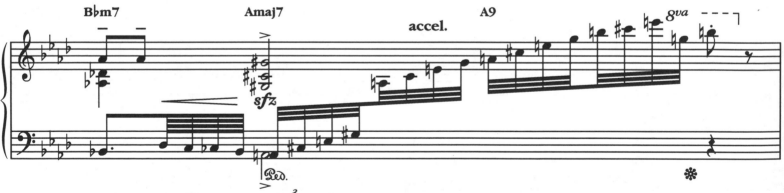

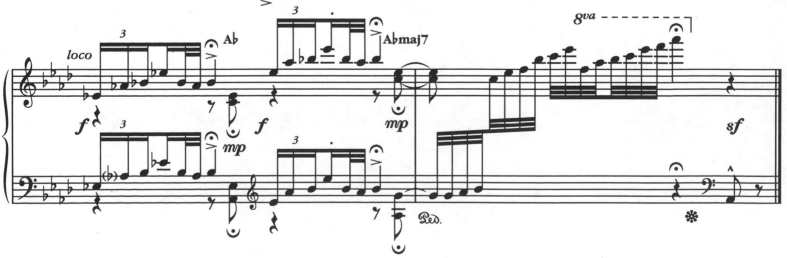